"*When Faith Becomes Sight* is an invita⸺⸺⸺⸺⸺⸺⸺⸺⸺⸺⸺⸺⸺⸺ in daily life. Beth and David Booram guide Christ-followers on a multi-dimensional spiritual adventure, enabling readers to experience the shimmering moments and sacred threads of God hidden as priceless treasures in what many see as mundane moments of life. This resource is biblically faithful, spiritually formative, historically grounded, and psychologically sound. In short, it is a gift."

Terry Wardle, professor emeritus of practical theology at Ashland Theological Seminary, founder of Healing Care Ministries

"If you have ever pondered your ability or willingness to slow down and notice God around you, you may simply need a nudge from a trusted guide to help open your eyes. The Boorams are such guides and offer wisdom for finding God in all things. With an invitation to linger, their writing not only gives permission for the contemplative in each of us to slow down and simply be present but to also move toward wonder and anticipation with God."

Whitney R. Simpson, author of *Holy Listening with Breath, Body, and the Spirit*

"With the rich fruit of years of Beth and David's companioning others in soul attentiveness, *When Faith Becomes Sight* glistens with wisdom and shimmers with the ways of our self-revealing God. Winsomely illustrated with examples from the Scriptures and from spiritual conversations and offering thoughtful reflection questions that help the reader to live into the invitations of each chapter, this book becomes its own burning bush experience!"

Susan Porterfield Currie, director of Leadership Transformations' Selah Certificate Program in Spiritual Direction

"*When Faith Becomes Sight* is a modern-day *Practicing the Presence of God* for those of us who aren't vocationally washing dishes in a monastery like Brother Lawrence. . . . This is a field guide to cultivating a mysticism in the mundane, the power of God always present and at work at your fingertips."

Ben Sternke and Matt Tebbe, copastors of The Table, cofounders of Gravity Leadership

"Beth and David masterfully and creatively awaken our deeper longings for an authentic relationship with God. Offering insights and practices from their own experiences as spiritual directors, this book is a gift to all of us who desire not only to grow in awareness of God in our day-to-day life but also to help others do the same."

Mike Bowden, director of Evangelical Spiritual Directors Association (ESDA)

"A world full of noise and distraction dulls us to the subtle movements of God and our own hearts. Dave and Beth Booram have shared generously from years of accompanying others to invite us to an awakened, discerning life. This book is like being in the room with them as they creatively guide us to a world-contradictory, God-responsive life."

Scott E. Shaum, associate director of Barnabas International, author of *The Uninvited Companion*

"It's all too easy for us to lose track of God's presence with us in our daily lives, especially when we are blinded by trauma, grief, or other challenges of life. Beth and David Booram are wise and hospitable guides who use stories from their many years of spiritual direction to show us how to recognize God's presence with us. By calling our attention to the Giver of all life, *When Faith Becomes Sight* is a life-giving book, one that will undoubtedly transform the lives of all who read it."

C. Christopher Smith, senior editor of *The Englewood Review of Books*, author of *How the Body of Christ Talks*

"*When Faith Becomes Sight* lovingly calls us with tender care yet intense focus to awaken all our senses to discern God's presence and activity in our lives. It is an ongoing work that requires us to stay in tune with what is happening within and around us as we cultivate our capacity to *be still and know* how God is working in our midst. This book is a gift to anyone who is ready to take the next step of seeing God anew and, in the process, seeing oneself anew as well."

Leah Gunning Francis, author of *Ferguson and Faith: Sparking Leadership and Awakening Community*

"This book isn't just about the life with God, it is something I have rarely experienced: *When Faith Becomes Sight* is spiritual direction in book form. It is a companion on the journey, a reminder of the ways God speaks and moves, an encouragement when times are dark, and a reminder that we all need a soul friend (or two) who will point us to the sparks of the divine within and around us at all times. I will return to it often, and I encourage you to, as well."

Tara Owens, spiritual director and founder of Anam Cara Ministries, author of *Embracing the Body: Finding God in Our Flesh and Bone*

"Beth and Dave Booram are experienced and trustworthy guides for exploring the complex landscape of the inner life. *When Faith Becomes Sight* is an honest, gentle, and engaging invitation to become increasingly attentive to the God who sees us with love. Filled with practical insights and opportunities for prayerful reflection, this book facilitates a journey deep into the heart of God. I hope many will say yes to the journey."

Sharon Garlough Brown, author of *Shades of Light* and the Sensible Shoes series

WHEN

Opening Your Eyes

FAITH

to God's Presence

BECOMES

All Around You

SIGHT

Beth *and* David Booram

An imprint of InterVarsity Press
Downers Grove, Illinois

InterVarsity Press
P.O. Box 1400, Downers Grove, IL 60515-1426
ivpress.com
email@ivpress.com

InterVarsity Press® is the book-publishing division of InterVarsity Christian Fellowship/USA®, a movement
of students and faculty active on campus at hundreds of universities, colleges, and schools of nursing in the
United States of America, and a member movement of the International Fellowship of Evangelical Students.
For information about local and regional activities, visit intervarsity.org.

Unless otherwise indicated, all Scripture quotations are taken from the Holy Bible, New Living Translation,
copyright ©1996, 2004, 2007, 2013. Used by permission of Tyndale House Publishers, Inc., Carol Stream,
Illinois 60188. All rights reserved.

While any stories in this book are true, some names and identifying information may have been changed to
protect the privacy of individuals.

Cover design and image composite: Cindy Kiple
Interior design: Daniel van Loon
Images: group of yellow blurry lights: © Torjrtrx / iStock / Getty Images Plus
        gold brush strokes: © MirageC / Moment Collection / Getty Images

ISBN 978-0-8308-4663-4 (print)
ISBN 978-0-8308-4837-9 (digital)

Printed in the United States of America ∞

InterVarsity Press is committed to ecological stewardship and to the conservation of natural resources
in all our operations. This book was printed using sustainably sourced paper.

Library of Congress Cataloging-in-Publication Data
Names: Booram, Beth, author. | Booram, David, 1955- author.
Title: When faith becomes sight : opening your eyes to God's presence all
    around you / Beth A. Booram and David Booram.
Description: Downers Grove, Illinois : IVP, an imprint of InterVarsity
    Press, 2019. | Includes bibliographical references.
Identifiers: LCCN 2019029419 (print) | LCCN 2019029420 (ebook) | ISBN
    9780830846634 (paperback) | ISBN 9780830848379 (ebook)
Subjects: LCSH: Faith. | Vision—Religious aspects—Christianity. |
    Spirituality—Christianity.
Classification: LCC BV4637 .B66 2019 (print) | LCC BV4637 (ebook) | DDC
    248.4—dc23
LC record available at https://lccn.loc.gov/2019029419
LC ebook record available at https://lccn.loc.gov/2019029420

P   25   24   23   22   21   20   19   18   17   16   15   14   13   12   11   10   9   8   7   6   5   4   3   2   1

Y   36   35   34   33   32   31   30   29   28   27   26   25   24   23   22   21   20   19

TO OUR FALL CREEK ABBEY COMMUNITY
of spiritual directors whose deep
and loving presence is helping others
see with the eyes of the heart.

AND TO THOSE WHO HAVE INVITED US
to accompany them as spiritual directors
as they seek to discern the presence
and action of God in their lives.

In order that an experience have a religious dimension two things are necessary: God who can be encountered directly and a person who is on the lookout for God.

WILLIAM BARRY, *SPIRITUAL DIRECTION
AND THE ENCOUNTER WITH GOD*

CONTENTS

PREFACE

THE DOORBELL RANG ABOUT 11 A.M. one Tuesday morning. I (Beth) opened the door and welcomed Rick into the foyer of Fall Creek Abbey, our home and retreat house. I'd met him before, but this was the first time that we would meet for spiritual direction. Seeing him again reminded me of my previous impressions—that he was a gentle, soft-spoken, kind man. I asked if he'd like a cup of coffee or tea. "No," he responded. "I'm fine—already had my quota."

I showed him to my office, a small room off the living room. Rick sat in the chair opposite me, looking out the window into our backyard. We took a few minutes to exchange small talk. Once I sensed that he was comfortable, I asked how familiar he was with spiritual direction. He explained that he'd heard about it for some time, liked the sound of it, and because of all that was going on in his life, felt it was time to seek some support.

We began with a brief period of silence in which I suggested that Rick ask God to help him identify what he should focus on during our time. He agreed. I watched as he bowed his head and closed his eyes. I did the same, praying silently a simple prayer of dependence.

Finally, Rick broke the silence by beginning to speak. His voice was soft and speech was slow. He told me about the last several years as the senior leader in a nonprofit organization. He was chosen for this role after a tumultuous season when the founder was asked to resign. For the first few years Rick felt empowered and energized by the work and confident in God's calling. Yet for the last year and a half, he'd begun to wonder if he was really the man for the job, if he really had what it took to do the job well.

This wasn't all, Rick explained. He'd had some health issues that made him feel fatigued and not himself. One of his adult kids had struggled with depression, and he didn't know what to do or how to help. And his prayer life; it felt empty, meaningless and dry. It hadn't always been that way. But for some time, he'd begun to wonder where God was for him. Why God seemed so silent and distant. He processed out loud how this stage of the Christian life wasn't what he'd expected. And he was at a loss as to how to make sense of everything.

I listened intently, praying to discern which thread of his story to give a tug. I finally asked, "Rick, if you were to say in a sentence or two why you're here today, what would you say?" He paused for a long moment. And then he said, "Even though I'm disappointed with God and life, and God seems so far away, I still want to be close to him." His eyes glistened at this admission. I nodded my head, feeling the integrity of his response. "Rick, what if the very longing you feel is an indication of the Spirit at work, awakening you more fully to God?"

Rick's countenance lightened a bit. He confessed that it was something he'd never considered. "If that were true, Rick, what might that reveal about how God is being toward you right now?" Again, he took his time to answer. And then he said, "It feels a little frustrating. I wish he would just show up and speak clearly or do something for me rather than just make me feel so desperate for him."

"Yes. That's understandable." I responded. "Why might God want you to feel so desperate for him? Is there anything in your desperation that might be important to experience?" This time, there was no pause. He blurted out with more conviction, "I think my desperation for God is making me seek him more than ever—more than anything. I think *that's* probably a good thing, right?" He grinned.

"What do you think? Is it good?" He exhaled a reply, "Yes. It's good. I guess it even feels good to want to be closer to God in a way that I haven't for a long time."

This conversation, though specific to Rick and his life situation, had a familiar ring to it. Not only did it remind us of the many stories we've heard in hundreds of hours spent in holy listening, it also resonated with our own lives and experience of God. We are two people who know what it is like to feel disillusioned, to struggle because the Christian life we're experiencing doesn't match what we had pictured life to be as a follower of Jesus.

EYES TO SEE

We've written this book out of the harvest of more than four decades of following Christ and a decade's time of offering spiritual direction. We hope you will benefit from the generous framework we offer—one large enough to hold the things that are perplexing, disturbing, and incongruent with reason and rationality. In short, rather than trying to fit God and life into a system of beliefs, this book suggests that we can find God by paying attention to our own lived experience, that we can, as St. Ignatius said, "find God in all things." Not that God *causes all things* but we can discover God present and available to us in the midst of all. To do so, what we need most are *eyes to see* God.

At first, that statement sounds as though some of us have "it" and others don't. As if some willfully choose blindness over sight. But our observations suggest that most people truly want to know whether God is present and active in their lives. So the lack of seeing is not out of stubborn refusal but rather out of simply not knowing what to look for or not recognizing unfamiliar expressions of the presence and action of God—like desire and desperation, as Rick discovered.

The intent of this book is to help you gain assurance that God *is* with you and *is* actively involved in your life and world by growing three capacities: your capacity to *recognize* God, *reflect* on your experience, and *respond* faithfully to God's presence and involvement in your life.

Here's a brief description of what we mean:

Recognize. There are two things that must be true for you to recognize God. God must want to be experienced *and* you must be looking for God. For the divine to be experienced, your encounter will invariably be mediated. In other words, God will come to you through something else: a "burning bush" in nature, an inner quiet prompting, a dream or vision, an evocative Gospel story, a recurring theme, or through some much-needed provision. The medium is not always tangible, but it is *sensory*. In other words, through your human senses, including your emotions, you perceive God through the experience. So, for you to recognize God you must have eyes to see God and expect to see God through a variety of holy, ordinary, and sometimes extraordinary showings.

Not only is learning to recognize God's mediated presence necessary for your assurance, so is a repeated experience of God's presence. When you have an experience, it is never isolated or simply episodic. It is an experience that builds on the past. You recognize an oak tree because you've had a past relationship with oak trees in which you noticed their particularities and logged their appearance in your library of botanical memories. The same happens *when faith becomes sight*. Through repeated noticing of God, your faith is strengthened as you become more adept at identifying Christ's invitations and overtures of love toward you.

Reflect. Once you gain the skills to track the Spirit's movement in your life, you will learn the value of reflecting on your experience. Reflection takes time. Reflection requires intention. Reflection is what takes the encounter into you, allowing it to affect you, to find a place of resonance within you. It's what allows an ordinary event in your life to become deeply personal, spiritual, and transforming. These kinds of experiences deepen your assurance of God's nearness as they become windows through which you see the activity of the divine.

Respond. Not only will you be encouraged throughout this book to learn to recognize God's presence within and all around you and reflect on your experiences, you will also be prompted to notice your response to God in your experiences. We are rarely aware that as we perceive God's initiating presence we also respond to it with some variation of openness or resistance. Paying attention to your response will help you assess if that is how you want to respond. If that is what it means for you to respond faithfully and fully to God's initiatives.

Rick had an initial reaction to God when he realized that God might be in his desperation. He felt frustrated. Why didn't God make it easier on him by being more deliberate in his actions or by speaking more clearly? Fortunately, once he reflected on his desperation, he began to see the gift in it. His desperation and the feeling of God's silence or absence made him want God more, thirst for God more earnestly. And in that increased thirst, he developed a more resolute surrender to his desire for God and commitment to seek God alone.

A word about how this book is organized. It's divided into three sections and will invite you to consider your experience of God through three distinct directions of focus: *looking for* certain phenomena in your experience of life, *looking through* several conscious and unconscious lenses you may have, and *looking within* your own interior life of emotions, sensations, and spiritual movements. May these three vantage points help your faith become sight as you open your eyes more fully to God's presence all around you.

Part One

LOOKING FOR:

RECOGNIZING

SIGNS OF GOD

God comes to us disguised as our life.

PAULA D'ARCY

SHIMMERING ATTRACTIONS

We saw His star, and we have followed its glisten
and gleam all this way to worship Him.

MATTHEW 2:2 *THE VOICE*

WHEN I (DAVID) TURNED FIFTY, I was reflecting on where I'd come from, who I was, and where I was going. I come from a long line of artists, and though I had always deeply appreciated visual art, I had never explored my own talent (or lack of it). So I shared this with Beth, who, in her typical noticing way, gave me a certificate for an art class at a local community art center. I discovered quickly that each day I had an art class was the best day of the week, and that I did have the seeds of some latent talent I could access.

One portrait class I took was taught by Ellie Siskind. I vividly recall my struggle throughout the course to represent mouths and noses, expressions and gestures. Yet the one thing that stood out from Ellie's instruction was her use of cadmium red as an underpainting technique. Cadmium red has a slight orange-like hue that almost vibrates when you see it. Ellie would underpaint her portraits with the color and then cover over 99 percent with the natural tints of the subject. The small amounts of the red that remained around the edges or were allowed to break through suggested vitality, energy, life. Even though not central to the painting, the red's presence excited.

A shimmering attraction in the spiritual sense has a similar quality. It might be a common object, scene, or sound, or it might be infinitely rare. Yet like the striking effect of this artistic technique, God draws our attention to something in our life. He animates the inanimate. And its presence excites.

Sometimes these shimmering attractions happen on the road you've taken a thousand times or through the window you've looked out every morning as you make the coffee. Suddenly, though often subtly, something lifts from the scene before you with inexplicable prominence. It might not be unusual at all, or it might be quite extraordinary. Whatever it is, for some reason you are drawn in, drawn toward this glistening point of interest in order to take a closer look.

TAKE OFF YOUR SANDALS

One of the most poignant examples of this type of God encounter in the Bible is the story of Moses and the burning bush. At the time it happened, Moses was watching his father-in-law's flock of sheep. One day, he decided to lead them into the wilderness, choosing a path that curved toward Sinai, the mountain of God. The hot, dry climate lent itself to wildfires, usually caused by lightning strikes. So, as he approached and noticed a bush engulfed with flames he might have formed an initial rational explanation. Yet something about what he saw provoked him enough to take a deeper look.

Read slowly this first-person perspective we've crafted based on the biblical account in Exodus 3:1-6, paying attention to the scene as it progresses, noticing what you notice:

> One crisp morning I was shepherding my father-in-law's flock of sheep as I did on most mornings. For some reason, I guided them far away from the usual paths and pastures to the other side of the desert and came to a place known as Horeb.

As I approached a small bluff there, a special messenger of the eternal One appeared to me in a fiery blaze from what looked like a bush. I did a double take, blinked the sand out of my eyes, and peered at the bush, but to my amazement the bush wasn't consumed by the inferno. I thought to myself, or to be honest whispered out loud to no one in particular, *Why's this bush not burning up?* I instinctively moved closer to get a better look.

As the eternal One saw me approach the bush to observe it, he addressed me by name and said, "Moses, Moses!" You can imagine how shocked I was, but cautiously whispered, with eyes closed now, "Here I am." Then I heard the words, whether with my ears or in my spirit, "Take off your sandals and stand barefoot on the ground, for now you know I am here and where I Am *is* holy ground."

Was the bush on fire, yet not burning? Or was the Presence within the bush afire with dazzling brilliance? Suddenly, it doesn't matter. Whatever the source of the shimmering, Moses was accosted by this unanticipated sight in which he encountered the Lord in the middle of this flaming shrub! What do you notice as you read the story? Does anything provoke curiosity, a question, or spark new insight related to this familiar yet strange scene?

Here are a few observations:

First, notice how Moses seems inadvertently drawn toward the wilderness on this path that led to Mt. Sinai. Though a lot of Old Testament history will happen later on Mt. Sinai, at this point, Moses would have had no sense of that. Isn't it curious that he was prompted to take an unfamiliar path to a place that would become saturated with significance to him and to Israel in the not-too-distant future? (Remember, Mt. Sinai is where Moses met with God for forty days and received the Ten Commandments.)

Second, observe Moses' amazement at what he saw. Though his brain could have provided a rational explanation, he seemed to know immediately that there was something extraordinary about this flaming bush, a "cadmium red" quality about the fire that shimmered even though the bush was not destroyed.

Did you see the effect this shimmering attraction had on Moses? He was drawn toward it, convinced that he needed to move closer, to pay closer attention.

Finally, once God saw Moses approach the bush to observe it more closely, God called to him by name. God spoke—once he was assured that Moses noticed the shimmering attraction and was walking toward it to give this curiosity his full attention.

This encounter can make us wonder how many times we walk by a "burning bush" and don't bother to notice it, our curiosity doused before its spark can take hold. How often do we see a glint of something that catches our eye but fail to slow down or stop and approach because we're in such a hurry, so pragmatically absorbed in what we're doing or where we're going? It is the paradox of revelation and mystery that we encounter in a shimmering attraction yet too often fail to recognize and move toward for a better look.

BEDAZZLED

The phrase *shimmering attraction* suggests light, reflection, movement. When you encounter an object or scene or sound of this nature, it interrupts your normal consciousness and what you're doing or thinking about. It grabs your attention, whether it's as small as a firefly, as subtle as an unfamiliar birdsong, or as encircling as a double rainbow. Generally there is an aspect of beauty; however it may be humble beauty in a garb quite unremarkable.

Shimmering attractions seem to take you by *surprise*. You don't seek them; they seek you. When encountered, they cause an inner double take: "Hey, what was that?" "What did I just see?" And yet they also seem a bit ephemeral to your normal consciousness and can be easily dismissed or ignored. You may circle back to it a few times, being gradually drawn into it as its deeper and personal invitation registers with you.

They also have an *alluring* quality. They draw you in, begging for closer examination, for deeper reflection. Shimmering attractions arouse your curiosity as they lift off the page of your life like a highlighted phrase or sentence, drawing your attention and registering with importance. In fact, the word *shimmering* is often used in contemplative literature to explain *lectio divina*, an ancient way of listening to God's personal word in Scripture. In the first movement of *lectio*, we are often instructed to listen for the word or phrase that shimmers.

It's also not uncommon for there to be an element of *place and timing* when you encounter one of these divine displays. You find yourself at the right place, at the right time, under the right circumstance. For Moses, it was simply another day as he shepherded his flock near Mt. Sinai. But it was also a time when God was increasingly grieved by the oppression of the Israelites in Egypt and moved to initiate action because of their cries of distress. God lit a fire to get Moses' attention, to ask for his help in delivering the Israelites from their harsh enslavement and to lead them into their own fertile and spacious land (Exodus 3:7-8).

One final note about these shimmering attractions: They often deliver the personal message "*God sees me.*" Unlike encountering a transcendent moment (discussed in chap. 3), which opens us to see God in a new and expansive way, this particular beacon of light transmits a signal that actually confirms to us that just as "God's eye is on the sparrow, so his eye is on me." For that reason, these encounters are particularly meaningful because you come to know experientially that *you* are seen by God.

Though each shimmering attraction has its own unique presentation and is its own unique experience, the nature of each will share some or most of these qualities. See if you recognize them in the following example as it happened in the life of one of Beth's directees, whom we will call Terri.

A SLIVER OF MOON

Three o'clock a.m. is a dreadful time to be awake. Terri agonized as she considered the conundrum: the amount of sleep up to this point wasn't enough for the day ahead, and the amount of sleep left to the night, if it came, would leave her groggy and in a stupor. So she finally gave in and slipped stealthily from her bed, hoping not to wake her husband or the dogs. Unfortunately, the latter were on to her.

Terri made her way, dogs in tow, to the kitchen, where she opened the sliding glass door to let them out. Immediately her attention was arrested by a sliver of moon squarely in her line of sight. This moon, more than three quarters obscured by darkness, left evidence of only a squint of the sphere. Terri gazed at it, lingering with its presentation, something so alluring to her that she couldn't look away.

Quietly and without fanfare a gentle thought formed in her mind. *This is how you see things. You see only a small part. I see it all.* The thought registered soundly with her. It addressed something she knew about herself, of her tendencies to judge life situations on partial knowledge, giving way to fear and feelings of intimidation. The words she heard were not sharp or condemning. They didn't shame or rebuke or chastise. They were spoken simply and gently. She knew they were for her. And she suspected they were from God.

Terri carried this experience with her for several days, continuing to reflect on its meaning and the general sensation it left her with. She wondered at the fact that the moon only presents itself as a sliver at certain times of the lunar cycle and directly in view from her back door only during this particular season. She also considered her waking from a deep sleep for no apparent reason. Was God's Spirit subtly nudging her to wake up? Was God drawing her toward something he wanted to speak through? *Does God do that?*

As we processed this experience together in spiritual direction, Terri was fully assured of God's presence and action through this crescent luminary. She shared her experience with me in a calm, confident way and with deep gratitude. After all, the God of the universe, the One who created the moon, had leaned toward her to convey something that he felt was important for her to know.

Since this encounter, Terri has noticed that when faced with something happening in life that is overwhelming or not according to her plans, the memory of this incandescent image reminds her that she only sees a small sliver of what is happening. The effect has helped her open more fully to God and trust the One who sees her and the One who sees all.

RESPONDING TO A SHIMMERING ATTRACTION

So how do you respond to an experience of a shimmering attraction? What do you do with it? These questions, so natural to our analytic minds, are likely the wrong ones. It's possible that God is inviting you to a new experience of the divine, and so God's changing the channel, so to speak, by initiating in a way that you can't fully explain or control. In a word, this shimmering attraction may be cradled in mystery. And what should you do when you encounter mystery?

You linger. You slow down and stay with what you've encountered, becoming present to it with all your being, senses, and spirit.

You contemplate. As you linger, you take a closer look by allowing that which has drawn your attention to be the singular focus of your attention, letting it be what it is and taking it in.

You wonder. You simply let the questions that emerge within you rise up. You release your need for answers or insight. You allow yourself to marvel, *How is it that among all the billions of human*

beings on this planet I deserve to be so personally addressed in what
seems a hand-picked moment?

You bow. You allow the encounter to humble you, to shape your
posture into one of meek receptivity. Rather than taking control of
the experience, you simply say, "Speak, your servant is listening"
(1 Samuel 3:10).

You follow the thread. At times shimmering attractions will be
complete and contained at the moment. At other times, they will
be a part of a thread in the seam of the fabric of life's journey—one
that other new invitations from God will come through. Like the
magi, you see the first shining of his star and then echo their words,
"We saw His star, and we have followed its glisten and gleam all
this way to worship Him" (Matthew 2:2 *The Voice*).

God longs to grow your sensitivity and responsiveness to these
sparkling harbingers as you move through your life's particular geography and approach each day willing to be interrupted by a
burning bush. One way you can practice paying attention is to
reflect on the past—the last few days, weeks, or months—and consider whether you've had any experiences that now resemble what
we've described as a shimmering attraction. Here are some questions to help you explore whether it may have been God initiating
with you through this means of revelation. (And by the way, we
encourage you to process this exercise and others in the book with
a spiritual friend or mentor, or in a small group. Something important happens when we use our own words to speak out loud to
others what God is inviting us to consider and notice.)

What experience(s) have you had recently that reminds you of a shimmering attraction?

Pick the most prominent one and then recall what stood out to you when you first noticed this alluring signpost.

What in your life needed to be addressed by God through this encounter?

How would you describe your experience of God through it?

How did you react initially to God's revelation?

How is God inviting you to respond now?

CHAPTER 2

RECURRING THEMES AND SYMBOLS

You know how to interpret the weather signs in the sky,
but you don't know how to interpret the signs of the times!

MATTHEW 16:3

OUR CHRISTIAN SCRIPTURES, like all sacred writings, are rich with themes, motifs, and symbols. These beautiful icons account for much of the timeless attraction and gifts that generations of people receive from them. Unfortunately, we can become so familiar with the narratives or so immersed in the actual history that we cease to see these enduring patterns that are relevant to our spiritual journey today. Recorded by those whose lives were enriched by them, these timeless threads invite us to notice and consider their current meaning, as well as identify other themes running through our own lives.

Many metathemes emerge again and again throughout the story of God in Scripture: life, death, resurrection; the land, the mountain, the sea; home, exile, and return. We also encounter more concrete motifs that connect with our simple, ordinary lives: fish, bread, seeds, water, wine, trees, and stones. All these themes are echoed again and again, often in a new context with new and refined meaning, but their repetition alerts us to pay attention. We are returning to a refrain that resonates with the holy.

Consider Simon who became the apostle Peter. Who doesn't know that before all else he was a fisherman? You can easily imagine Peter's childhood home, the aroma of fish on an open fire, the smell of fish oil on his father's hands and scales stuck to his beard. Think of the first time his father asked Peter to come with him on the open sea to learn the trade and picture the delight when together they pulled in his first haul. Fish were in his dreams and in his blood.

Peter's initial recorded encounter with Jesus centers around his occupation. He's fishing with his brother Andrew and their partners James and John. They've had a disappointing night; not uncommon but frustrating when your livelihood depends on it. Jesus, who'd been speaking to a growing crowd at the shore, swings into the boat and encourages the fishermen to set out to the deep waters again. Reluctantly they agree, and after he directs them where to put down their nets, when they draw them up they find they are overflowing with the biggest catch of their lives!

As they're bringing the fish ashore, perhaps reveling in all they'll be able to do with the excess profits, Peter oddly tries to send Jesus away, as though overwhelmed by what had happened. Jesus, not put off by Peter's words, sees into Peter's heart. He invites Peter to follow him so that Jesus can show him how to cast another kind of net into the sea of humanity, instead of the Sea of Galilee.

Several of Jesus' miracles pick up the fish theme. With five thousand hungry souls to feed, he enlists Peter and his friends to feed them. Confused, they confess they don't have the means to provide for such a large crowd—though they could likely calculate how many catches of fish it would take. Instead, Jesus takes the small meal of fish and bread from a young boy and deepens the meaning of the motif. The Lord of the fisherman is also the Lord of the feast.

Peter heard parables about fish and saw a coin taken from the mouth of a fish, not to mention the connecting events involving boats, and nets, and the sea and its storms. The theme continues and deepens, even after the resurrection. When Jesus appears to Peter and the other apostles in the upper room, they are dumbfounded, wondering if he's a ghost. To prove he is real, Jesus asks if they have anything to eat. They give him a piece of fish.

The culmination of Peter's encounter with this symbolic icon is recorded in John 21.

> The disciples, in spite of the experience of encountering the risen Christ, are restless and untethered. So much has happened and they are struggling to make sense of it all. In a moment of what seems like muscle memory, Peter calls out and tells them "I'm going out to fish." Several follow, returning to what was familiar or what used to be familiar before Jesus upended their lives. It was a long, unremarkable night, filled with empty silence and no fish.

> As the sun comes up they notice a solitary figure on the shore. This stranger calls out to them and asks about their catch. They shrug their shoulders and admit that it's been a long, unproductive night. The man encourages them to cast their nets on the starboard side of the boat and assures them that they will have better luck. They do, and once again, like a recapitulation of an earlier net-breaking catch, they drag in a monstrous haul. Peter and his friends immediately realize it's Jesus!

> Peter jumps into the water and hurries to the shore while the others bring in the boat and the fish. Stunned and bewildered, he looks around and notices a small charcoal fire with fish and bread on it. It smells delicious and the warmth of the fire begins to warm his wet, stiff body. Jesus, having prepared it for them, asks them to collect some of the fish they'd just caught and set them on the fire with his. As the fish sizzles on the coals, Jesus takes some and offers it to his disciples.

As they sit together eating in silence, Jesus puts his hand on Peter's arm and steers him away from the circle. He looks into Peter's searching eyes and asks him; "Do you love me more than these?" *These what?* Peter must have wondered to himself. *These friends, these boats, these* fish? Three times Jesus asks the same question, and Peter, unsure what Jesus is fishing for, answers, "Lord, you know everything. You know that I love you."

Some years later, as the early Christians were being persecuted and some even martyred for their faith, they sought a secret symbol to indicate their allegiance to Jesus. The sign they chose was the simple, unambiguous fish. "Do you love me more than these?" Indeed.

WEAVING PATTERNS

Recurring life themes and motifs, like in a musical composition, are repeated encounters with the same or similar words, ideas, places, stories, songs, experiences, dreams, or symbols that add structure and unify our lives. They weave the disparate parts of your life into a single garment that embodies beauty and design. Noticing them is a valuable practice because they acquaint you with your particular and peculiar soul and lead you toward your unique path of life. When you encounter these patterns, you're reminded of places you've been and lessons you've learned about yourself, about your life, about your God.

It might be helpful to take a moment and differentiate some terms that we're using. First, a *theme* speaks of the "big idea" of a story or musical composition. It tells us what the story or composition is about. *Symbols* are images that represent larger themes and more abstract ideas, like a dove for peace or a skull and crossbones for poison. And a *motif* is a repeating pattern that reinforces a theme. So, while we might use these terms interchangeably, each one does represent a unique idea. Your life is composed of large themes, often represented and reinforced by unique symbols and motifs that are personal, distinctive, and give structure to your life story. What meaningful symbols or motifs come to mind right now? How do they reinforce the major emphasis of your life?

I (Beth) have noticed a life theme emerging through a recurring dream. This nighttime fantasy happens at least yearly, if not a couple of times each year, and I've had it now for more than thirty years! In the dream, I'm either pregnant or have just had a baby. Or sometimes my mother is pregnant, or someone in my dream whom I don't know is pregnant. Or I'm wondering if I'm pregnant but unsure. Or I'm supposed to be pregnant but I don't look pregnant and worry that the baby has died. As I reflect on this recurring dream, it most clearly speaks to me of my yearning to create and give birth to the new. Because of the demands of a large family, my particular vocation, and my own personality bent, I've often given all of my energy to caring for the needs of others. My creative self expresses its longing through these symbolic dreams, awakening me to the need to express myself through birthing and creating.

RESONATING AND REVERBERATING CHORDS

As we've learned from Peter, symbolic icons act like strong chords connecting the events of our lives by helping us find their meaning *if* we are attentive to them. But how do you recognize these substantive chords? Jean-Marie Howe describes what happens within us when we encounter symbols. She suggests that "there is a vast interior space within the human person where the reality signified by the symbol or image can reverberate: this space is what we have been calling the deep *heart*. The *heart* harbors unfathomed spiritual depths of infinite resonance."

Both the words *resonance* and *reverberate* are terms describing different sound effects and are keys to recognizing what happens when we encounter important symbols. Howe suggests that our hearts are like an acoustical chamber where certain signs, symbols, or images seem to strike a chord. They reverberate; they resonate.

By noticing the sensation of resonance we can identify the symbols that strike a chord with us.

But why? Why that symbol or motif? Why does one person find meaning in the recurring experience of seeing a great blue heron, and it means nothing to someone else? Why is the ocean a symbolic and nostalgic place for some, and others are drawn to mountains? Because themes, symbols, and motifs are *uniquely personal* and give clues to who we are in our deeper self and what gives substance to our lives. Howe goes on to say, "Symbols and images serve to awaken the *heart*, causing it to vibrate and resonate, thereby signaling, to all who have ears to hear, the presence of unsuspected or neglected spiritual spheres inherent in human nature." You recognize a mean- ingful symbol because it resounds within you, *awakens your heart* to unknown, hidden depths you didn't know existed.

Another quality that helps you identify important recurring images and experiences is the way they invite you to *return* to previous times and experiences. Like the motif in classical music, these elements provide a structure to the music of your life. They are important touchpoints that help you connect the past with the present and cul- tivate hope for the future. They remind you that you've been here before, that this is a familiar place and you know how to find your way.

One of the recurring themes in our lives has been the consistent experience of being "called away" from one thing before we are "called toward" something else. This repeating pattern has happened every time we've made a significant move or change. It begins with a growing restlessness or yearning for something more or different, even if there is no apparent reason to seek a change. The hard thing is that we initially have no clarity about what that something more or different is. We will simply feel no longer settled where we find ourselves. This experience is hard to explain to others because it's so deep and intuitive and not founded on anything other than a vague disquiet and drawing away.

Once we open ourselves to this now familiar experience and allow our hearts to awaken to it, we eventually get some clues about where or what we're being called toward. Recurring symbols and themes like being called away before being called toward do that for us; they awaken our hearts to a new horizon by giving us courage from our past. As you begin to track these recurring patterns, they will help you see each leg of your journey, not as a random happenstance but connected by a thread woven throughout your past, present, and future.

As an example, listen in on David's conversation with a directee, Chris, and see how a recurring symbol has become a unifying theme in Chris's life and kindled a compelling vision for his future.

A RIVER RUNS THROUGH IT

I (David) have known Chris for nearly twenty years now. We originally met at church and after we left that church we lost track of each other. Then not long ago we reconnected through his professional expertise as a consultant. As I shared with Chris about spiritual direction, he was intrigued. Chris was approaching retirement age and was anxious to discern what this season of life might hold for him and how God might be pursuing him in it. So we began to meet monthly for spiritual direction.

Several months later, Chris arrived one morning, walked directly to the coffee station, and picked out his favorite mug—the one with the picture of a trout in a river bed—and filled it with coffee. We walked upstairs to my office and sat down. He thanked me for coming to his mom's visitation. She had recently passed away and I hadn't seen him since then.

As we settled in I prayed for our time together and then asked him what it was like to be on this side of the loss of someone who'd been part of his entire life's journey. After a few minutes of pondering (Chris is a self-proclaimed ponderer), he spoke the words "Grateful. Blessed."

Somehow I sensed that God was inviting Chris to review his life with a deep sense of its gift. He then went back in his mind to his growing up years, his frequent visits to his grandparents' farm, and the freedom he had as a boy. There was a river, he told me, that ran near the property, and that became his spot. It had always drawn him. He closed his eyes, returning to the smells, the sights, the sounds. He recalled how his mom would call him home; how he felt the strong sense of her presence and her love for her family. "She was a strong and faithful current in my life, just like the river. And so was Dad. They're both gone now, but something of them is still flowing through me."

This was not the first time we'd talked about "the river." Like a musical motif, it would come up every so often over the months we met. It had become a common reference point in our conversations, often as Chris was seeking to make connections and see where God was at work, or what God was showing him. His most native spiritual practice was to walk to a river near his home. Drawn to it in all kinds of weather, he would stand on its banks and ponder his life. He also had shared that when he traveled to a new place, he would intentionally seek out a new river or stream. There was something in his soul that needed the grounding of this theme of moving water contained within those banks.

We pondered together the movement of his life a bit more, and as he looked up with misted eyes, he quoted, "'When peace like a river, attendeth my soul.' That's what I feel. Though I miss Mom and can't imagine where I'd be without her, I have peace, and it's the same peace I feel when I'm at the river."

"It sounds like this river has been a source of many good gifts, Chris," I reflected back.

"It is, just like my life. God has brought so many good things to me that I don't deserve. I'm not sure why I'm so blessed, but that's the only word for it."

"Chris, I wonder if the river is inside you now. Like the rivers of living water that Jesus says can be ours. You carry the river inside you, and just like you were nourished by your mom, it's now your turn to be the river for others."

He was silent for a minute and then said, "Even though I'll be officially retired in a few months, I still want to offer my gifts and my time to people who might need me. My kids and family, for sure, but I want to be part of whatever God brings along for me to dip my toe in. If it's my turn to be the river for others now, that would be a double blessing."

As I remember Chris and his pondering, I can't help but think of the closing lines from Norman Maclean's *A River Runs Through It*—a story rich in recurring themes and an invitation to notice and be grounded in our own themes that have hold of us. The final line names those themes as a haunting. Not a fearful, ominous haunting, but a haunting that is an echo of the divine Composer's enduring heart toward us. Hear the final words from this beautiful scene:

> Like many fly fishermen in western Montana where the summer days are almost Arctic in length, I often do not start fishing until the cool of the evening. Then in the Arctic half-light of the canyon, all existence fades to a being with my soul and memories and the sounds of the Big Blackfoot River and a four-count rhythm and the hope that a fish will rise. Eventually, all things merge into one, and a river runs through it. The river was cut by the world's great flood and runs over rocks from the basement of time. On some of those rocks are timeless raindrops. Under the rocks are the words, and some of the words are theirs. I am haunted by waters.

RESPONDING TO RECURRING SIGNS

Though recurring symbols and motifs are often unplanned encounters, you can intentionally participate in rhythms that naturally center you in a thematic flow of time. Consider the Christian liturgical calendar in which we engage the returning themes of Advent, Christmastime, Epiphany, Lent, Easter, and Ordinary Time. By grounding your life in these yearly repeating patterns and themes, you are also directed on your own pilgrimage toward your journey within the journey of following Christ.

When engaging with the unplanned symbolic encounters mentioned earlier, we recommend the following adapted exercise, suggested by David Benner in his book *Sacred Companions*. Benner offers this approach for the purpose of probing the meaning of a dream, but it can effectively apply to recurring themes, symbols, and motifs, as well.

- *Title.* Begin by giving the recurring image, symbol, or theme a title. It can literally be the symbol's name, like "Fish," as in Peter's story.

- *Theme.* Note your impression of the theme or meaning of this returning icon or experience as it relates to your life. What does this symbol remind you of? What similar experiences or encounters does it connect with in your past?

- *Affect.* How do you feel when you encounter this sign? How do you feel now as you prayerfully reflect on this symbol or theme and its meaning for you?

- *Questions.* Note any questions that this symbolic encounter surfaces for you. What does it make you inquisitive about?

Finally, our last suggestion for responding to a recurring symbol or theme is to bring it into your living space. Make something, buy something, wear something, or collect something that reminds you of this recurring theme and its importance to your life. Place it in your home or on your body (think jewelry or even a tattoo!) in a notable spot so you see it, which reinforces its meaning every time you do. Let the seeing strengthen the unfolding poem of God within you (Ephesians 2:10).

Can you identify any recurring themes, symbols, or motifs in your life? What comes to mind?

What does this symbol awaken in you? How does it resonate or reverberate within you?

What deeper truths does it surface? What new gifts are being brought out from the depths of your heart?

What have these recurring themes and symbols meant in the past? What do they mean now?

What might God want to remind you of through them?

CHAPTER 3

TRANSCENDENT MOMENTS

Even as he spoke, a bright cloud overshadowed them,
and a voice from the cloud said, "This is my dearly loved Son,
who brings me great joy. Listen to him." The disciples
were terrified and fell face down on the ground.

MATTHEW 17:5-6

I (DAVID) SETTLED INTO MY OFFICE CHAIR, iPad open on my lap, and initiated the Skype call. I'd learned from experience that a virtual platform can facilitate an unusually focused, robust, and intimate conversation with directees. So I wasn't surprised when, once again, this proved to be the case with Deborah. We took time to catch up on her recent vacation and some minor health challenges she'd been navigating. Then after twenty minutes or so, our session headed in a very significant direction.

Deborah had just shared about a situation when she'd become the center of attention and how difficult that was for her. I wondered to myself about how she felt being the center of God's attention. So I asked her, "Can you recall an experience when you felt that you were the center of God's attention? A time when you felt God's eyes on you?"

Without hesitation, she began to tell me the following story:

One summer evening in Vancouver, while studying for a final in a course on prayer at Regent College, I was unexpectedly interrupted by an intense and pervasive idea to go outside. This was not procrastination. This idea did not originate with me. There was something "calling" me outside, and I didn't know what it was. I simply had to get up from my desk, leave my room, walk down the hall, and step outside. And so I did.

Once outside I looked around, and to my left, off in the distance, I saw three tall, slender evergreen trees forming a kind of triangle. Somehow I knew this was where I needed to go. I walked over and stood in the middle of these trees and looked up. Several moments passed, and then quietly, as though time was standing still, I felt the sensation of being encircled by the Trinity: Father, Son, and Spirit. Surrounded, and embraced; welcomed and delighted in. I don't know how long I stood there. But I know that when I finally left, I felt different. I was marked by the encounter.

I walked back into the dormitory, and as I passed my friend Sharon's room, she called out to me. I turned, and when she saw my face, she exclaimed, "What happened to you?" I fumbled to find the words to tell her what had happened. And then she smiled and said, "God kissed you!" Yes. Yes, that is surely what happened. Though this occurred thirty years ago, it was and is one of the most moving and memorable gifts I've received from God in my lifetime.

While the phrase *transcendent moments* may conjure images of ecstasy and rapture, these experiences with the sacredness of someone, something, or some place that take you beyond the horizons of your current awareness may be encountered in ordinary events like Deborah's. These are moments when for a brief period of time you are transported beyond yourself and your current frame of reference. They awaken you to God in and beyond the veil of temporal existence and remind you of the magnitude and mystery of the Creator and Sustainer of life.

The literal meaning of the word *transcend* reinforces the kind of experience we're describing. It's created from the composite of two Latin roots, *trans* (across) and *scandere* (climb). Together they suggest to climb across or climb over or to rise above. Consider the stories you've heard of people who've described having an out-of-body experience. They die on the operating table and view the whole scene of being resuscitated from above the table looking down until they eventually rejoin their bodies. For a moment, they transcend the thin veil between earth and heaven, between the temporal and spiritual realms. That's often what a transcendent moment feels like: an out-of-body, time-standing-still, spiritually charged experience.

Consider these vignettes as other examples of sacred, transcendent moments:

Hearing the first vulnerable cry of their newborn daughter, a couple huddles together, staring at her with wonder, their vision blurred by tears. Time stands still. They look at her and marvel, "How could this be? She's truly a miracle!"

A young man reaches the summit of a mountain after a rigorous climb and gasps at the panoramic view. He turns around ever so slowly, taking in as much as he can. His heart pounds as his mind tries to comprehend what registers intuitively—that something, Someone—is holding together everything he sees.

Seated in a grand hall, absorbed in the glorious swell of sound from the orchestra, an elderly couple clasp hands and are transported to what feels like heaven. Their souls are rocked by the cradle of this immense love they feel—for one another, for life, for exquisite music and this beautiful shared moment.

One of the most memorable transcendent moments for me (Beth) happened in the fall, many years ago, during a difficult time in my life. My heart was heavy, truly breaking, from some hurtful conflict within my church community, where I served on staff. One evening as I drove back to church for a meeting, heading north on an open road, I became aware of a warm light to my left. I then made a left turn (west) and was instantly blinded by the source: before me blazed a brilliant sunset with warm colors streaking on either side of the horizon. The sun actually looked so enormous it was almost eerie in size. In fact, it appeared that if I kept driving I would drive right into it! It literally took my breath away. As my heart lifted in a spontaneous response of worship, very clearly and yet quietly, I heard the Spirit of God whisper to me, "I'm bigger than all of this." I will never forget the consolation I felt as I received those words into my heavy heart.

WHEN THE HEAVENS OPEN

Not only is our life punctuated by these occasional sacred experiences, but Scripture is also a record of ordinary people like us who periodically encountered life-defining, transcendent moments as well. Jacob wakes from a mysterious dream about angels climbing a ladder to heaven and exclaims, "Surely the LORD is in this place, and I wasn't even aware of it!" Isaiah sees an astonishing vision of God seated on a throne with seraphim calling out to each other, "Holy, holy, holy." Or recall the poignant reunion between Mary the mother of Jesus and her relative Elizabeth. Mary, having just conceived Jesus, visits Elizabeth, who is also pregnant with a son, John the Baptist. Immediately John leaps inside Elizabeth's womb, and she is filled with the Holy Spirit. Elizabeth knows instantly that "the mother of her Lord" has come to visit.

One of the more dramatic and classic transcendent moments in the Bible is included in all three Synoptic Gospels: Jesus' transfiguration. Can you imagine being Peter, James, or John when Jesus comes to you in private and invites you to take a walk with him up a high mountain? Follow along with this narrative of the event as though *you* are experiencing, first-hand, this remarkable scene that takes you beyond the veil of temporal reality into an experience of eternity.

Jesus has just asked you to go with him to the top of a steep mountain. You feel excited and special to be chosen. And a little unsettled because this is a bit out of the ordinary for Jesus, and he really doesn't explain anything to you.

After a strenuous climb, you finally arrive at the summit. The view is spectacular in spite of the fact that the wind is bone-chilling. You turn slowly around to take in the entire scene and then notice in your peripheral vision light radiating from your right, from where Jesus is standing. You turn and are astonished to see his face glowing beyond description. His clothes look as though they've caught fire they're so dazzling white. And then you realize that he's talking with someone. Two people, actually.

Visible to you are two other figures, people you intuitively know are Moses and Elijah, and they're having a conversation with Jesus. If this isn't enough, Peter is saying something about building three tabernacles when unexpectedly a large, shimmering cloud overshadows and envelopes all of you. A Voice speaks out of it; a Voice like no other you've ever heard. You fall face down to the ground, stricken by fear and trembling as the Voice speaks: "This is my dearly loved son, who brings me great joy. Listen to him."

Still with head buried, afraid to move, a gentle hand touches your back. Jesus says almost apologetically, "Get up. Don't be afraid." He can tell you're rattled to the core. You look up and see no one except him. *What just happened*, you think to yourself? There are no words to explain or categories to frame this experience. But you know for sure that you will never, ever forget what you saw and felt. And it will certainly be for you a significant touchstone on which your faith returns whenever you have doubts.

While we may never experience anything as dramatic as Jesus' transfiguration, even a less dramatic transcendent moment can leave us speechless and with the same awe and assurance of God's "with-ness" and immensity. Consider some traits of these faith-altering occasions and compare them to your own encounters with God's transcendence.

FROM CHRONOS TO KAIROS TIME

Common to many experiences of God's transcendence is an initial sense that time has changed or stopped. You might name it as *a transition from chronos time to kairos time*. Chronos time is clock time, time that can be measured or ordered, as in the word *chronology*. Kairos time is about moments—moments when everything stands still as if life is holding its breath. It's what we call a "pregnant pause" because, though it's empty space, it's also full of possibility. In the transfiguration scene that's what happens when suddenly Moses and Elijah become visible to you; it's like you're seeing beyond the temporal into the way things are in eternity.

Another feature of transcendent moments is your heightened awareness of the *sheer magnitude* of God. The mountain climber drinks in the panoramic view and declares that the expanse is being held together by Someone vastly bigger! Deborah felt embraced by the eternal, immortal Trinity in the space created by three magnificent trees towering above her. And Jesus and the disciples, enveloped by the shining cloud, sensed their earthbound selves viewed from the expansive kingdom of the One whose voice they heard.

In addition to their magnitude, *mystery* forms the shadowy edges of transcendent experiences. While the immensity of God is awe-inspiring, the mystery that *is* God takes you beyond your treasured comfort zones. Transcendent moments expose you to those aspects of God that are unknowable and unsearchable. The enigmatic essence of this transcendent One can be disconcerting. Maybe that explains Peter's awkward and impulsive offer to build shelters for Jesus, Moses, and Elijah. What else do you do when you're confronted with something your mind can't wrap around?

Finally, transcendent moments speak to your need for *reassurance* that life has meaning. As a human, you are a meaning-seeking creature. You wander through life hoping to snag sufficient evidence that who you are and the life you're living really do have some purpose, some beauty, some meaningful design. This innate drive influences you to try to make sense of life's circumstances, your relationships, your conflicts, and your life work. Transcendent moments often reassure you that life indeed has meaning because God is solidly and purposefully involved in your destiny. That Jesus "is before all things, and in him all things hold together" (Colossians 1:17 NIV). God sees you—and because you are seen by God, you know that you matter to him. Transcendent moments reassure you, in the words of fourteenth-century anchoress Julian of Norwich, "All shall be well, and all manner of things shall be well."

ENTER QUIETLY

A recent trip to Muir Woods in Northern California brought that reassurance home to us. It felt like a sacred pilgrimage. As we entered Cathedral Grove, we absorbed the sign that simply read "Enter Quietly." Slowly walking amid these twenty-five hundred-year-old giant redwoods, a sort of sacred hush descended in the atmosphere. As I (David) went on ahead, I saw a young man pause, reach out his hand and reverently place it on the rough bark of one of these ancient living monuments soaring nearly three hundred feet above us. I was thankful for his unhindered example. His simple gesture increased my desire to be open to this place and this moment. The peace that surpasses understanding can be breathed here. I continued on quietly grateful.

As I exited the area, still absorbing the surrounding wonder of it all, I found myself walking behind a young woman who was clearly agitated. Her friends yelled back to her asking what was going on. She held up her broken sunglasses, upset that she'd dropped them, splitting them in two. Her friends waited for her to catch up and then asked what happened. She started laughing and said, "I dropped my glasses as I was watching this video—you guys have to see it. It's so hilarious!" They surrounded her small cell phone screen, laughing together at its trivial entertainment while above and around them stood weighty witnesses to a world that existed before Christ.

RESPONDING TO THESE CRACKS IN THE UNIVERSE

How can you respond to these cracks in the universe that offer you a glimpse of heaven? How can you avoid being hijacked by petty distractions so you don't miss out on glimpsing the magnitude of God and God's overtures of love and affirmation?

You open yourself to the possibility. To become open to a transcendent moment is to develop what could be termed double vision. We live much of our days with our eyes turned downward, hands fixed to the grinding wheel. Our momentary relief often comes from trivial distractions and empty pursuits like a video on a cell phone screen. At least within that circumference we are masters of our universe, albeit a very small one indeed. To recondition our way of being, we must be open to the possibility of transcendence, "lift our eyes to the hills," and look for our helper and maker.

You pay attention to kairos time. Transcendent moments are by definition episodic and infrequent. It's not possible in our current order of being to experience wave after wave of perpetual transcendence. Were this the case, it is unlikely we would be stirred to feed ourselves or the hundred other things life requires of us as human beings inhabiting this world we call home. And yet these moments originate and unfold as if they were from a completely other realm.

We can neither manufacture nor control them. They simply cannot be programmed or domesticated. But we can pay attention to them when they happen by becoming familiar with and noticing those stand-still moments of kairos time.

You wade into the wonder. When we stand near one of these graced and transcendent cracks in the universe, our capacity for celebration and wonder will then be seen as the only fitting response. As Maximus the Confessor says, "Only wonder can comprehend his incomprehensible power." When we enter this hallowed space that transcends temporality, we must hold our breath and wade into the marvel of it. We will then be prepared to sing with all sincerity the psalm of the seraphim: "Holy, Holy, Holy! The whole earth is full of your glory!"

Transcendent moments serve as a bridge from where you currently are to somewhere beyond. The human experience for all eternity will be one of moving toward ever-expanding, ever-new horizons within the ultimate reality of God. As an adult believer, you are invited to move through this world with a more relaxed grip called faith and acclimate to this grand adventure that takes you beyond your current understanding and grants a true taste of abundant life and infinite love.

Take some time now and reflect on your own experience of transcendent moments. Scan your memory for times when you were ushered into the hush of God's grandeur and felt the reassurance that comes from knowing that all is well and all manner of things are well in your world.

When have you experienced a transcendent moment that took you beyond your current understanding and experience of God?

Can you recall the setting? What had been happening in your life before this experience that gave it context?

What was it like? What did you feel?

How did you react initially? How did you ultimately respond? As you think back, do you wish you would have responded differently? If so, how so?

What meaning was offered to you through spoken or unspoken words or impressions?

How are you being addressed right now by this graced moment?

CHAPTER 4

SLENDER THREADS

Keep on asking, and you will receive what you ask for.
Keep on seeking, and you will find. Keep on knocking,
and the door will be opened to you.

MATTHEW 7:7

SEVERAL YEARS AGO, pastor and author Brian Zahnd was in Paris the same day that postmodern philosopher Jacques Derrida died. He read the news while in route from his hotel to the Cathedral of Notre Dame for a presentation on the history of the cathedral. Arriving early, Brian headed across the river to the English bookstore Shakespeare and Company to buy something to read on his way back to his hotel, forty-five minutes away by train. He selected a paperback copy of *The Idiot* by Dostoyevsky—a rather impulsive purchase given the fact that he had a hard copy in his hotel room!

Brian sat through the presentation about the history and construction of the Notre Dame Cathedral. There was little in the presentation of spiritual significance, yet the transcendent effect of this Gothic architecture was still quite moving. He sat still for a moment at the end of the lecture and prayed a simple, yet sincere prayer: "God, use me more in this city." And then he left, boarded his train, and began to read *The Idiot*.

A young man sat across from Brian, noticed what he was reading, and commented on it. Brian asked if he'd ever read *The Idiot*, and the young man said, "Yes. I'm reading it right now." "Really?" Brian queried. Eventually, Brian asked what he was doing in Paris, and the young man explained that he was backpacking across Europe, having just graduated from college. "That's fabulous!" Brian added. "What's your degree in?" The young man shared that he'd graduated with two degrees, one in political science and the other in world history. "Impressive!" Brian responded.

They talked further about other books and authors important to this young man, and then Brian asked a formidable question, "So, you're young and have your whole life and work before you. What hope do you have for the world?" The young man paused and then quietly admitted, "I have no hope for the world." "Really? That's sad," Brian replied. Then the young man took the lead and said, "I heard that Dostoyevsky was a 'born again' Christian." Brian, knowing well the story, confirmed the rumor and filled in more details about Dostoyevsky's life of faith.

Finally, the young man asked curiously, "What do you do?" Brian smiled and explained that he was a pastor. "Well, since you're a pastor, I'll tell you my story." The young man proceeded to share how he'd grown up Catholic but lost his faith in high school and became an outspoken atheist. Yet he came to Paris and decided to go see the Cathedral of Notre Dame. "When I got to the cathedral and walked in, I knew there was a God. So I prayed to God. I told God I was sorry. But I don't think God heard me."

"Really?" Brian responded. "You don't think God heard your prayer? Even though we just happened to sit across the train from each other? And truth be told, I just bought this book, *The Idiot*, in spite of the fact that I have a hard copy of it in my hotel room, so that you might see it, remark about reading it, and we would talk together?" The young man lingered with Brian's comments, then fixed his gaze on Brian and asked, "Would you pray for me?" Brian said, "Yes, of course." And he did. Then suddenly, Brian looked up and saw that he was at his stop, said goodbye to the young man, and the train whisked him off.

SLENDER THREADS

Current science seems to be catching up to what stories like this one illustrate and spiritual traditions have known all along: we live in a unified and whole universe held together by a living, connective tissue. We are not simply fragmented and isolated entities belonging to a random, incoherent world. From time to time, this interconnectivity presents itself, and we, for a moment, pause, noticing the unlikeliness of the startling confluence. And if we are open, we find ourselves wondering what meaning, invitation, provision, or warning it might carry for us. How might God be pursuing us in these unusual and arresting events?

Terms such as *synchronicity*, *serendipity*, *providence*, and others have been added to our lexicon to help describe these not so uncommon marvels.

You have a chance meeting with a perfect stranger who sits next to you on an airplane. That conversation is an answer to prayer and leads to an important affirmation to continue in a new direction you'd been contemplating.

You stumble onto several resources through a chain of events— a book, a mentor, a podcast, an article—that provide the very help you need to face a challenge you are suddenly confronted with but had no idea you would be facing.

You've been stuck for some time, unable to make an important decision, when you come across the same message in the line from a song, a verse in Scripture, a comment of a coworker, and a card you just received from a friend. All of them together help you know what to do.

You begin to dream about writing a novel when you find a random postcard tucked inside a library book advertising a fiction writing class in your community.

Perhaps you've experienced similar moments and still puzzle over their significance and meaning. To better grasp these experiences, consider these three words—*synchronicity, serendipity*, and *providence*—and what they are describing.

Providence is an older term that recognizes, often in retrospect, that there was a watchful, benevolent intervention that supplied something needed or steered one away from destruction toward blessing and life. It's not difficult to see the gracious and merciful hand of God in these moments. Providence provides what is lacking and what we cannot take credit for manufacturing on our own.

Serendipity originated from an eighteenth-century fairy tale where the heroes in the tale experienced a positive confluence of events simply by chance. The emphasis is on the surprise, the wonder, the fun of it all. It could have some deeper meaning, although it often may not. It may be experienced simply as a "happy accident," as artist Bob Ross puts it.

Of these three terms, *synchronicity* could be considered the more technical and precise. This is in part because it was coined by Carl Jung, a serious student of how the human psyche and the human experience worked together to help make meaning of one's life. Consider these descriptions:

- the uncanny and fortuitous timing of events that go beyond pure chance
- a meaningful coincidence
- a confluence of circumstances beyond human engineering that are encountered as God's effort to gain our attention or provide something we need

- Specific outward signs or circumstances that seem somehow to answer our inner needs, wants, or questions

In his memoir, *Balancing Heaven and Earth*, Robert A. Johnson's story is principally an inner journey guided by powerful dreams, visions, and synchronistic events. Johnson's account is a curious mixture of his persistent awareness of the external realities of his life and the irrefutable intersection of unseen, benevolent provisions. After sharing repeated examples from his long life, he concludes that "this type of synchronicity has occurred so many times that I now take it as a principle that whatever I need will turn up if I am patient and have the awareness to perceive it. These turns of fate have been so unpredictable and yet so wise that they are beyond any intelligence that my ego might claim."

Johnson's preferred term for describing God's providential involvement in his life is a *slender thread*. For him and for us these slender threads carry specific meaning regarding the needs, wants, and questions we carry inside us whether we are aware of them or not. "I think that the slender threads are continually present, it is just our ability to accept them that varies."

A PROVIDENTIAL WELL

Though none of these specific terms appear in Scripture, the experience is portrayed often in narratives that illustrate how these slender threads have guided, encouraged, and warned our spiritual ancestors. Through these uncanny moments we watch their trust and hope increase as they witness with their own eyes that they are not alone as they seek to be faithful to the journey they're traveling.

That's certainly the case in the story of this unnamed servant who is sent by his master, Abraham, to find Abraham's son Isaac a wife. Read the following story based on Genesis 24 as experienced from this man's perspective.

My master, Abraham, has been a kind and generous man to me and my family for nearly fifty years. His stories of how his God called him by name and guided him through his long life have been an inspiration to me. They've often nurtured my small faith as I have sought to be faithful to this God that he knows so well.

Not long after his wife of many, many years died and he too was showing the weariness and weakness of his old age, he called for me to visit him in his tent. He seemed more frail than ever, but there was the fire of one final concern that burned in his eyes: a wife for Isaac from his own people and country. Taking my arm in his boney grip, he both begged and commanded me to put my hand under his thigh and swear that I would by no means arrange for a marriage with any of the local women but rather travel back to his homeland and find a suitable wife from among his own relatives.

My love for my master and commitment to his concerns were real, yet this responsibility was heavy on me. For my trust in his God was not as tested as his. Yet I knew I must do this thing he asked of me and that I must also trust his God and mine as never before. So I prepared ten camels laden with expensive gifts and offered up a prayer that I would be alert and responsive to the ways and blessings of God. And thus we set off on the long, difficult journey.

When at last we arrived, we came to the well on the edge of the town of Nahor. It was nearly dusk and the women were coming to draw from the well. The camels knelt down to be watered and I too knelt with both my knees and my heart and prayed, "God of my master Abraham, please make me successful today and show your loyal love to my master. You see me as I am kneeling here by the spring as the young women of the city are coming to draw water. Let the one who responds to my request for water be the one you have chosen for your servant Isaac."

It is beyond me to know how all these things happen so gracefully, but as soon as I was finished praying, a young girl approached the well. I watched her for just a moment and then wasted no time and asked her for a drink of water. She agreed and even offered to water my camels. As I gazed at her in silence, I waited and wondered if she could be the one I was meant to meet. It felt presumptuous and yet also hopeful.

When I finally roused myself, I asked for her name. She told me it was Rebekah. I asked who her father was and if there was room for us to spend the night. She told me that his name was Bethuel, son of Nahor, and I immediately recognized him as Abraham's kin. Rebekah assured me that there was plenty of room and even straw for the camels.

I was overcome with gratitude. She must have wondered at me as I bowed my head and worshiped this One who had not failed to show his loyal love and faithfulness to my master and had led me directly to my master's relatives.

Rebekah and Isaac have been married almost five years now. My master Abraham has gone to be with Sarah and his God. I serve Isaac and Rebekah much like I did Abraham, but now his God is truly my God. I have seen with my eyes how he blesses and guides me through prompts that help me follow the slender threads that I encounter along the way.

What a simple, straightforward, yet beautiful example of God's providence. At one level it's about a father's concern for his son, who needs a wife. At another it's about the desire of a faithful friend and servant to fulfill his master's request. At still another, it reveals God's delight in ordering the inner and outer prompts that bring about his purposes and grow in us the delight of living in a world where trust makes sense and faith becomes sight.

Are there any useful observations for our lives that we can glean from this story? First, this providential encounter began with this servant's *commitment to take action*. Without that commitment, nothing much would have happened. There would have been no movement, no awareness of need, no openness and observance. As W. H. Murray suggests, "the moment one definitely commits oneself, then Providence moves too."

And speaking of commitment, God's providence occurred not as Abraham's servant waited but as he *stepped out*. Something is activated when you get out of your chair and walk toward life. As you are going, initiating, living into what you do know, you begin to look for what you need in order to make progress. After all, Jesus commands us to ask, seek, and knock. "Everyone who asks, receives. Everyone who seeks, finds. And to everyone who knocks, the door will be opened" (Matthew 7:8).

Finally, *prayer plays a significant role* in this story. Without prayer, you tend to stumble along, feeling alone, and succumb to self-sufficiency and self-determination as your life's default mode. Prayer prepares your heart, your mind, your eyes, and your ears to notice when the slender threads appear. Prayer awakens you to your needs, longings, and questions so that when you finally are addressed, you notice. And prayer strengthens your commitment to not compromise along the way. *How might you pray differently so that when the slender thread of synchronicity appears you are prepared to engage with it?*

NOTICED BY GOD

Jessie is a single woman in her late thirties who's been on quite an adventure for the last several months. It all started a year ago when she went to Cambodia with a small care team from her church. The purpose of the trip was to support a band of frontline missionaries working in the sex trafficking industry by offering them soul care through facilitating a retreat and providing spiritual direction.

Jessie had never done anything like this before and was awash with fear *and* excitement. And the trip proved to be life-changing.

During her time there, Jessie discovered her real passion for young women recovering from such horrific abuse. This led her to resign from her job as a teacher and begin raising support to return to Cambodia and work there full time. Jessie and I (Beth) had been meeting for spiritual direction for a couple of years. In fact, Jessie had also gone through our School of Spiritual Direction training we offer and was now providing spiritual direction to a few others. It was thrilling to companion her during this time of intense spiritual awakening and discernment!

During a session of spiritual direction, Jessie shared a surprising experience she had while reconnecting with an old friend. She was meeting with Becky to share her plans and to see if she would consider becoming involved financially in her ministry:

(Jessie) So, I met Becky for lunch at this restaurant near where I used to live right after college. I hadn't seen her for several years, even though she'd been a good friend. When I walked in, I looked around, hoping I would recognize her, and instead, I saw another face that looked familiar.

Instantly, when I made eye contact with this woman, I realized she was a friend from that era as well. Samantha looked at me with an expression of surprise—well, really more like shock—and then stood up and walked toward me with a huge smile on her face. "Jessie?" she responded. "I can't believe you're here! I was literally just talking to the friend I'm having lunch with about you. I was telling her that I'd heard about your courageous move to Cambodia—that's right, isn't it? And how much I'd wished I could see you before you left but was pretty sure you'd already gone!"

Samantha went on to tell me why she was eager to see me. She'd recently gotten a large bonus at work and felt like God was asking her to give some of it away. So, she'd prayed

and asked God to help her know who to give it to. Then later
that day, while at the gym, Samantha bumped into Becky—
the friend I was meeting for lunch. Becky told her how we'd
just reconnected and that we were going to have lunch. She
explained all about my plans to Samantha. At the time,
Samantha didn't connect her prayer when she asked God to
help her know who to give the money to. But later when she
put it all together, she felt concerned that she'd missed the
opportunity. Obviously, she hadn't!

By this point, Jessie's face was beaming. We sat for a moment,
savoring the gift of this slender thread of God's presence and providence, and then I asked her, "What touches you most about
this experience?"

Jessie was thoughtful and responded, "I'm just overwhelmed
by how God is going before me, preparing the way and providing
for me." I nodded and then asked, "What about that over-
whelms you?"

"It's just so personal and caring—so involved." She replied.

"Does that surprise you?" I queried.

"Yes. In some ways, it does. I'm not used to being so noticed by
God." Jessie added.

"Noticed by God ... what's that like for you to be noticed by
God?" I offered.

"Overwhelming and uncomfortable and, I have to admit, pretty
amazing," Jessie replied.

"Jessie," I ventured, "How do you imagine God is feeling toward
you as he watches you receive these gifts he has for you?"

Jessie exhaled, "Oh—wow. I've never thought about how God
feels toward me. I don't know ..."

I suggested that we sit for a few minutes in silence and that
Jessie pray and listen to God's response to the question. A few

minutes lapsed. I kept my head bowed and when I looked up, I saw a few tears trickling down Jessie's cheeks.

She finally spoke up and said, "God feels happy."

PLACEHOLDERS OF PRAISE AND GRATITUDE

One of the primary characteristics of this phenomenon we've just described as a slender thread is the remarkable nature of coalescing events. There's usually an element of *perfect timing*, such as "If I'd been there a minute before or a minute later, I would have missed it." Or a certain sense that these events simply could not have been humanly orchestrated. Though some are subtle and others more dramatic, we are convinced that these kinds of things are happening far more often than we realize. If you wonder whether you've experienced one of these actions of God in your life, consider whether it is exceptional in its quality or timing. And if it is, the most important thing to do is to be curious and open to what it has to say to you.

Another feature to notice is *the message it speaks* to your inner, unconscious needs, questions, or desires. The providential nature of a slender thread distinguishes it from happenstance because of the meaning embedded within this kind of experience. I (Beth) once woke from sleep one morning hearing a verse of Scripture playing across the soundtrack of my mind: "People do not live by bread alone, but by every word that comes from the mouth of God." This startled me because it had never happened before. As I sat with this experience, it eventually dawned on me that Jesus had repeated these words during his forty days of temptation in the wilderness. I knew instantly and intuitively that I was entering a wilderness and would also be tempted to lose faith. My premonition was realized within a few short months.

Whatever their remarkable nature or meaning might be, these providential moments are often *pure gift!* Like in Jessie's case, they buoy you and strengthen your faith that God is weaving your life together with purpose, significance, and connection. As you reflect on the slender threads woven within and throughout your life, be diligent to write them down. Some threads will be mute for a time and the meaning will not come for many days, months, even years. Keeping a journal of these happenings will ensure that you can return to them and keep listening for how God is speaking to you through them. Allow these meaningful coincidences to become placeholders of praise and gratitude.

RESPONDING TO SLENDER THREADS

When many of us hear of these surprising and unusual events, our inner agnostic leans toward one of two directions. Either we dismiss them as chance occurrences or we deny our worthiness to receive such concrete encounters from the demonstrative hand of the living God. It's certainly prudent to avoid viewing every occurrence in life as if it is filled with some deeper, hidden meaning. And yet why wouldn't we expect God to provide for us in unique ways that are beyond the usual modes of care? Should God want to meet our needs in such arresting ways, why would we deny the gift of God in them?

In the words of Sam Keen, consider how you might enter each day "with expectation that the happenings of the day may contain a clandestine message addressed to you personally. Expect omens, epiphanies, casual blessings, and teachers who unknowingly speak to your condition." What difference might it make if you approached the unfolding of your life with expectancy? How can you move toward life with anticipation that there are slender threads of connection, support, and provision for you to find? As you do, consider the following steps of response.

When you have an experience that reflects the qualities of a slender thread of providence, *give the experience time* to reveal its meaning or message. Don't rush to dismiss it or be too quick to claim it as from God. Simply give it time to unfurl the potential gift it holds for you. Be curious and open and prayerful, just as Abraham's servant was as he waited at the well.

If you receive confirmation that this is not happenstance but a provision of God, *receive it in faith as a gift*. Open your heart to the gift and allow it to awaken gratitude, and express your gratitude to God with genuine praise and adoration.

Finally, *tell a friend* about your experience. When we share our stories of God's care for us, the experience often becomes more real and our conviction deepens by talking about it. Revel in the details; savor the timing of it all. And don't be shy to lift up the light of God's providence for others to see. Their stuttering faith that these slender threads might exist—even for them—will increase!

As you reflect on your own life, are there any experiences that come to mind that remind you of synchronicity, serendipity, or providence? If so, what are they?

When this experience took place, how did you respond to it? What was your initial reaction?

Upon further reflection, is there anything else that God might want you to pay attention to? How do you want to respond now?

Since these experiences don't come to us as we wait but rather are encounters we have on the move, what dreams, desires, or purposes are you currently moving toward? What actions or steps are you resisting that might be important to take?

How might you pray differently so that when the slender thread of providence appears, you are prepared to engage with it?

CHAPTER 5

THE FERTILE VOID

The earth was without form, and void; and darkness was upon the face of the deep. And the Spirit of God moved upon the face of the waters.

GENESIS 1:2 KJV

I (DAVID) MADE THE QUIET DRIVE to the hospital. It appeared that Linda's health was rapidly declining and she would soon transition from this life into the next, death and life both holding her with equal grasp. As I sat and prayed with Linda, we enjoyed a few quiet moments together. I stood up to leave, about to say goodbye, when musical chimes started to play a lullaby. Like many hospitals, Saint Francis had a longstanding tradition to recognize the birth of a baby to patients throughout the wings with this simple and joyful reminder: new life enters even where sickness, pain, and mortality are most palpable.

Imagine a world without death. Imagine a world where nothing decayed and disappeared. Over time the entire surface of the planet would be covered with all that's come before. The shelves of nature's cupboards would be crammed with yesterday's produce. There

literally would be no space left for the arrival of new life, new cre-
ations, the realization of dreams and visions.

As much as we grieve, resist, and deny death, without these
losses, both literally and figuratively, our lives would eventually
become so crowded that we would be unable to wriggle free in
order to grow and change. Without the renewing and recycling
process of decomposition there would be no new supply of nu-
trients for building future life forms, both psychologically and
physically. Death, in fact, is not the last enemy. Our fear of death is.

AN OXYMORON

It's not uncommon, but is rare enough, that two seemingly opposite
ideas are juxtaposed in such a way that a new and richer meaning is
birthed. The words *fertile* and *void* are two that we typically would
not find together. They're what we call an oxymoron. And yet when
first encountered, the couplet seems to name a dark truth that our
soul may know but our mind has yet to accept and embrace. A void
is a place of emptiness, hollowness, or loss. When you experience a
void like this there is a visceral awareness of no-thing-ness; that
which once fully occupied your life, filled your attention, and composed even your sense of self is no more. It's as if you've been stripped
of a source of vitality and meaning and left alone with no
apparent replacement.

Consider these common experiences of void:

- loss of a job
- death of a loved one
- declining health, aging, or debilitating illness
- broken relationship
- unanswered prayer
- nagging boredom

- disruptive move to a new location

- an unfulfilled dream

- embarrassing or devastating failure

- betrayal or isolation from a spiritual community

- loss of a title, role, or reputation

- vanishing stability or safety

- clinical or circumstantial depression

- deconstruction of theology or spiritual tradition

As you review this list, which ones resonate with your own history? How do you feel as you are reminded of your own experience of this foreboding vacuum? There's no way to sugarcoat it: the fertile void is not a place we willingly go. We a-void it!

WHEN MEANING-MAKING CEASES
AND BEING BEGINS

We both meet with the same spiritual director, Nancy, who introduced us to the concept of the fertile void. As a technical term (which we are not following strictly), it originates from Gestalt theory and was coined by psychologist Fritz Perls. He described it as an experience where "meaning-making ceases and being begins." Perls's definition describes how we experience a fertile void. Where once we might have tried to think our way through a situation to make meaning of it, now, recognizing the fertile void, we become keenly aware that all we can do is "be" in it and accept it for the dark mystery it is.

Although we've listed large and well-defined losses, the experience of a fertile void and its curious gifts are not confined to those ground-shaking devastations we encounter. Some are vague and only glimpsed initially in our periphery. The first time Nancy introduced the term to me (David), I'd shared with her about my weariness and lack of vision for a position I'd held for a number of years.

In and of itself the job was fine, but my heart just wasn't in it. As I struggled back and forth with the blessing and my ambivalence about the work, Nancy said, "It sounds like you're bored." I allowed the word to settle in, and it was as though something hidden, camouflaged by its surroundings, came into focus. She was spot on.

Nancy went on to share with me how boredom can be a sign of a phenomenon called the fertile void—an experience that has the potential to bring rich, new gifts to light. As I absorbed the presence of this lethargy in me, my first inclination was to shake myself and find a burst of energy to dissipate the malaise. Nancy patiently listened and then gently encouraged me to slow down. "The process of receiving the gifts of the fertile void," she explained, "will emerge organically and in their own time. If you willfully attempt to 'get through and get beyond' this time you will likely miss what has begun to ferment in the boredom. Let the boredom do its work and then respond with curiosity as you detect new life."

Throughout the biblical story there are many hints of this type of experience we're calling the fertile void. In the language of Scripture, it is sometimes called the valley of death, walking in darkness, or the desert wilderness. In these cases, the images describe a place of barrenness, an experience of aimless wandering in the dark or the sensation of lostness.

Many who hover at the edge of this daunting abyss would rather turn away. Most of the time they don't have the option. Yet in the story we will explore right now, this character *could* have taken an alternate route but chose instead to stay in his fertile void. Let's reflect together on the life of Joseph, Jesus' earthly father. Read the following imaginative account, told from Joseph's perspective just before his death, as he shares some life reflections he wants to pass on to Jesus.

Living Water from a Dry Well

Joseph found it harder to breathe today than yesterday. He'd never expected to become ill, to be dying at such an early age. He'd just asked Mary for a few moments alone with their son Jesus. The boy was growing taller now, and Joseph was proud of the way he looked their customers in the eye as he asked them what carpentry work they needed to be done.

As Jesus walked in, Joseph took his young, callused hand in his own and asked him to sit beside him. Even though Joseph knew that Jesus had been conceived by another Father, he had no trouble feeling that the boy was truly his son as well. Joseph took a deep breath and launched in, hoping to say what was in his heart.

"I know you've heard many times about the events surrounding your birth. I still think about them a lot. What I want to share with you is the dark but rich side of my faith, something that tested me deeply during those first few years. Your mother and I were betrothed and looked forward, like most young couples, to beginning a new life together. We dreamed of having a home that was ours and many children of our own.

"When I found out that your mother was pregnant—I hope this doesn't embarrass you—I was devastated. It felt like a stomach punch. Never had I felt so betrayed. I walked around in a depressed stupor until I finally went to see your mother. She told me again about how the angel had approached her and the Spirit had conceived you in her womb. I wanted to believe her, but it was so unlike anything I'd ever heard before. Then, through a dream, God spoke clearly to me and invited me to be part of the plan to care for and protect you.

"From that point forward there was a great absence of security and the comfort we had hoped for. We felt estranged from our families and the people of our village. Then the census was announced and we had to travel to Bethlehem about the time you were due to arrive. We were so young, so alone and frightened. We couldn't find a place to stay and in spite of God's guidance, you were born in a stinking stable. We barely had a place for your mother to lie down, and all I could do was pace in the dung. Even still, I was overjoyed at your birth!

"Then Herod learned of you through the magi and became obsessed with finding you. God warned me in another dream to escape to Egypt. You know how ordinary your mother and I are! We'd never traveled that far and had little money and even less experience. But we packed our few earthly belongings and headed out into the dark. Only later did we hear that Herod had sent his henchmen house to house to kill every male child born around the time you were. I felt so utterly broken and horrified by this atrocity. It made no sense. How could this be happening? Where was God in all of it? How could I keep you safe?

"As we waited in fear over the following years, we were uncertain if we would ever be able to return home. Eventually, after Herod's death, God spoke to me in yet another dream and assured me we would be safe to return to Nazareth.

"Those early years were filled with so many questions and so much darkness. Yet, even in the uncertainty of where we were going, God began to teach us how to trust him with the smallest, simplest things. We grew so much through our desperation and the inability to control our own destiny. I can't believe I'm saying this, but I wouldn't trade that time for anything. I'm telling you all of this because I want you to always remember that when you feel lost in a dark abyss and you feel that you are all alone, God's presence is with you, even though his movements might be hidden. And out of that dry, desperate well, you will soon draw living water."

Joseph often seems like a secondary character in the Christmas pageant, one that stands off to the side, lacking distinction. Yet, as we consider the events of Christ's birth through the lens of his own humanity, it's quite sobering to imagine how hard it must have been for Joseph to stay engaged (literally!), only having partial knowledge, only seeing a splinter of the whole of what was going on. Yet he did. He consented to enter and remain in this fertile void. He said yes to the darkness, the unknown, the uncertainty. And we are left to observe by his quiet, faithful presence that he was met by God in the void and changed by it.

IN LIMBO

So, how do you know when you're experiencing this phenomenon called the fertile void? Some might wonder if it's the same as "the dark night"—an experience we'll describe in part three. While there are similarities, a fertile void is different. Dark nights are experienced when we don't perceive God's presence or movement interiorly, but they are not necessarily tied to external circumstances. A fertile void, as we speak of it, is related to external circumstances involving absence, unwanted change, or loss.

So, the primary way you recognize a fertile void is that something inherent in your being *resists* the experience of it—for several reasons:

You resist the absence. Your initial reaction to a fertile void is to try to relieve the sensation of feeling empty, like when your stomach gnaws with hunger and you spontaneously react by filling it with food.

You resist the dimness. In the fertile void, you are unable to see what is happening or know what is going on. The experience feels dry or dark, not necessarily ominous but certainly unclear.

You resist helplessness. One innate quality of the fertile void is that there's really nothing you can do to alleviate it. The work that God is doing is hidden and mysterious. And God doesn't need your help. Shucks!

You resist feeling in limbo. In a fertile void you feel as though you are stuck in limbo, suspended midair and unable to bring closure to your situation. You can't rush to resolve it if you are going to allow the process to work it's magic.

You resist the inertia. Because boredom is often a symptom of the fertile void, it can cause you to feel anxious and desperate to overcome your sluggishness. Yet if Fritz Perls's description is accurate, one of the gifts you receive in this inert space is the capacity to *be*. You develop the capacity to be present, to be still, to be content, to simply be with yourself, with another, and with God.

Though we all have an initial aversion to the fertile void, once we consent to it, it is a powerful phenomenon that can free us from our compulsive drives, get us out of our heads, help us find our center, and learn to be! The following spiritual direction example illustrates the transforming potential when we consent to be in a fertile void.

A-VOIDING

I (David) have had the honor of accompanying several men and women into the fertile void known as retirement. I'm struck by seeing such capable and courageous individuals walk toward this finish line with strong, deep trepidation, only to circle back, again and again, before really crossing the line.

Max is one of those individuals. I started meeting with him shortly after he'd moved to Indiana from out west. He had family here and wanted to be close to his children and grandchildren. Max had been a senior leader of a fruitful ministry. He'd faithfully lived out his calling for several decades and now found himself slogging into retirement, struggling with any real sense of clear, defined purpose. For Max, this was the fertile void he had feared most.

When we first met, Max would reminisce about his previous role and what he liked about it, as well as what he found difficult. I recall asking him what was most challenging about being outside the fray of his former busy life. He looked off into the distance and said, "It feels like I've lost my whole way of life—my position, my role, my colleagues, and even the familiarity of the geography. It's all behind me now." As we continued to meet each month, I sensed him slowly loosening his grip on what he'd been trying to hold on to from his past and be open to being in the fertile void of retirement.

Over the next three years, Max gradually began to settle into his new life. He had gone through the Fall Creek Abbey School of Spiritual Direction training and some promising opportunities had opened up. He began offering spiritual companionship to a number of seminary students in Asia. In addition to that, he was writing resources for pastors in Africa and hosting conferences for them in their countries.

When we met recently, Max seemed more relaxed and at home. "How are you doing, Max?" I asked. "You know, Dave, I think I've turned a corner. I think I've finally retired from striving and grieving all that I've been trying to lay down. It feels good. And I'm feeling more settled here in our home too. I still don't know where it's all going, but I'm okay with that now."

"So what's stirring in you these days, Max?" I asked.

"I know for sure, that no matter what my role is, I'm a teacher and a pastor. And I'm getting to do that. Just in a form I hadn't imagined. I don't know if this is all there is, but I know that this is what I'm supposed to be about."

"Max, if you were to ask God a question right now, what would the question be?"

Max paused with his eyes closed for some time and then quietly spoke these words, "After all these years, Lord, are you going to give me the desire of my heart?" At that point, his head sunk and Max let loose and wept for several moments. A holy dam seemed to have burst, and I was at a total loss to know what was happening.

As I waited and prayed, he finally looked up at me. He told me how as a young man he'd felt called to Africa and had made an earnest attempt to serve there several times. After many twists and turns to his story, including a divorce and an aborted attempt at a PhD, he'd shrunk back from all traces of the dream. And yet now, after all these years, here he was standing on the runway of what seemed to be the fulfillment of his God-given dream.

RESPONDING TO THE FERTILE VOID

If the key feature that helps you recognize the experience of a fertile void is through your resistance to several of its uncomfortable features, the best way to respond is through your *consent* to allow God to transform and shape you through these experiences. What does that look like?

Consent to feel the absence. You befriend the experience of hunger, loss, absence, or deprivation. You discover the truth that you won't die because you don't have what you once had. There is sadness and grief in the loss, yet joy in discovering your own resilience.

Consent to walking in the dark. The prophet Isaiah instructs us:

> If you are walking in darkness,
>   without a ray of light,
> trust in the LORD
>   and rely on your God. (Isaiah 50:10)

In a fertile void, you don't have the luxury to sit and wait until the hand of fate returns what it has taken. You have to keep walking. Though you want to rely on seeing and knowing what's going on in the fertile void, you have to trust that God sees and knows what's going on.

Consent to feeling helpless. Transformation often feels like a free fall. The fertile void teaches you to let go of trying to manage what God is doing in you, to lay like a good patient on the operating table and let the good Physician perform his healing work.

Consent to the process. When you experience a fertile void, if you are to harvest the fruit, you must say yes to the time it takes for that to happen. Waiting patiently in limbo is a grace, for sure. Consenting to the boredom and inertia helps create a capacity for being present that will impact every dimension of your life!

THE POSTURE OF CONSENT

Our good friend Dana, a spiritual director and grief coach, was leading a centering time recently for a gathering at Fall Creek Abbey. Dana asked us to recall something in our life that we cared deeply about but seemed to be slipping from our grasp. She then asked us to physically make our hands into fists as if they were gripping and clinging to whatever came to mind. After a minute or so she invited us to open our hands and turn them palms up in an act of surrender, opening to the possibility that God might want to exchange whatever was in our hands for something as yet unseen. Our open palms became a symbolic posture of both offering as well as receiving. Finally, she asked us to turn our hands upside down toward the floor and make a motion as if we were releasing whatever was in our hands and letting it go, not simply surrendering it but relinquishing it.

This is the posture needed to respond to these unwelcomed, emptying experiences that descend on us as if out of nowhere. The posture of consent grounds us in the fertile void so we neither hang on to the past nor force our way prematurely toward the future, missing the gifts growing beneath the surface of this unique and uncomfortable landscape.

Can you identify a time when you experienced a fertile void? What was going on? What was it like for you?

When you were in the fertile void, what was your experience of God like?

How did you respond to this experience? Did you discover anything that's become important to you? Explain.

If you had a friend experiencing a fertile void, what advice would you give her or him?

What has been the good fruit of your experience of the fertile void? What did it teach you about being?

Part Two

LOOKING THROUGH:

DISCOVERING OUR

UNCONSCIOUS AND

CONSCIOUS LENSES

*The task of theology today is foremost a psychological and
anthropological one—to bring light into the darkness
of human existence by taking back the projections
of human fears and aggressions into the divine.*

EUGEN DREWERMANN

CHAPTER 6

THE FACE OF GOD

*God, who said, "Let there be light in the darkness," has
made this light shine in our hearts so we could know the
glory of God that is seen in the face of Jesus Christ.*

2 Corinthians 4:6

IN HIS BOOK *The Knowledge of the Holy*, A. W. Tozer observes,
"What comes to mind when we think about God is the most important thing about us." We remember reading this while in college
and how its compelling simplicity urged us on in our journey to
know God with as much clarity and integrity as possible. Something in us intuitively knew, and still knows, that if we get this
wrong, the effect will be dramatic!

As much as we agree with Tozer's observation, we now know
that it also needs to be expanded a bit. That's because in addition
to our conscious and scripted concepts about God, we have many
unscripted and unconscious notions about God. And it's these—
not our creeds and confessions—that largely control how we relate
to God and others, and live out the implications.

To add another aspect to our point of view, it's not just what *we*
think about God but equally important what we imagine God

thinking and feeling about us. As our good friend Dana said recently, "How we think about God is our theology. What we believe God thinks and feels about us *is* the relationship." This train of thought intuitively suggests that each of us has an internal library of unconscious God images that we've absorbed from our parents, community, faith traditions, culture, and life experiences. These have been imprinted on our psyches. And from this largely hidden collection we experience our soul's deeper orientation toward God, one that persistently tells us who we are to God and who God is to us.

OWNING OUR PROJECTIONS

Most of us have a basic idea of the human phenomenon known as projection. When we are projecting, we have taken some aspect of our own personality and imposed it on the other. We are hardwired to make sense of the world through our projections. Unfortunately, we rarely become conscious of them. Humanity's two favorite projection screens seem to be dogs and God. For instance, we project all kinds of human traits and experiences onto our pup, Bongo. Our recent favorite is to call him an "old man" (he's fourteen) as a way to explain his new proclivity to get on sofas (not allowed!) or his loud, urgent barking to let him out as a dropping of his well-mannered filters as an octogenarian. (When we're honest, he's never really had good filters.)

But beyond dogs and God, the truth is that the only way we see and know anything is as a form of projection. So, the problem isn't that we project but rather how closely our projection approximates reality, whether our projection reflects the true nature of that which we are contemplating. In relation to God, our spiritual director often reminds us that our image of God is not God but more accurately the God of our present understanding.

A number of years ago we were sensitized to the importance of recognizing our projections of God at a seminar for spiritual directors. Our presenter, Matthias Beier, a counseling professor at a nearby seminary, explained both clinically and theologically how certain unhealthy God images amplify suffering and violence, both individually and collectively. We were urged to take great care in remembering that our image of God is not one and the same as God.

"We see in a mirror dimly," Paul says. That doesn't mean we cannot see anything or know anything. It does, however, underscore that because of our weakened perceptions and the inherent danger of our projections, we must clearly discern whether our image of God is hostile or life-affirming. Images of God that are angry and against life must be seen for what they are: distorted images of God. They distort the reality of God. They distort how God relates to us and feels about us, which is best described as loving. "God is love, and all who live in love live in God, and God lives in them" (1 John 4:16).

How do you determine whether yours is a healthy or unhealthy God image, a hostile or life-affirming God image? Simply put, whatever engenders *fearful disapproval* reveals a radical and fundamental distortion within you. Whatever inspires *loving trust* points to your increasing proximity to the God who is. Are you afraid of the God of your understanding, or are you naturally drawn to surrender to Love?

Here are a few questions that might suggest the presence of a hostile God image:

- Does my God image pit God against me?
- Am I afraid of God?
- Does fear or guilt motivate me in my relationship with God?
- Does my God image make me ashamed of being human?
- Does it make me feel I'm not good enough as I was created?
- Does it ever fuel my self-hatred or hatred for others?
- Does it reinforce that God is untrustworthy and capricious?
- Does it make God out to be competitive and domineering?

In considering how a life-affirming God image might be recognized, consider this analogy. When someone whose job deals with currency is charged to recognize a counterfeit bill from an authentic one, they are trained to carefully note the minute features of a genuine dollar bill. There is an assumption that when people are trained thoroughly to know the real deal they will quickly and easily recognize an imposter. We wish that were true in discerning our God image. However, as we swim in the murky waters of our distortions, it's necessary that we learn to recognize both the impostor and the authentic.

Let's now consider a few questions that can help you discern the presence of a life-affirming God image.

- Does my God image help me see God as a loving companion of all humans, including me?

- Does my God image create and instill confidence and motivate me to loving trust?

- Does it encourage me to embrace my full humanity and vulnerability as well as that of others?

- Does it inspire me to see God as one who freely gives with no strings attached?

- Does it challenge me to grow into adulthood and live from my true self, able to both differentiate and experience intimacy?

- Does it reinforce my feeling that I am seen by God, felt by God, and safe with God?

- Does it convince me that God is utterly reliable, no matter what?

You see, when you functionally (whether stated or not) maintain a hostile God image, God is experienced as untrustworthy, punitive, distant, withholding, and bafflingly capricious. You can easily see how these distortions will yield a decreased capacity to draw near and attach to God. Only in relationship to and with the experience of radically unshakable love can you be healed. *In this posture of secure attachment, you become increasingly at home in both intimacy and autonomy with God and others.*

A JEALOUS GOD

Meredith and I (Beth) have met for two years now. She's a sensitive, creative, gentle soul and I look forward to our time together. A mother of three elementary-age kids, as well as being a preschool teacher, Meredith doesn't have a lot of time for self-care. Coming for spiritual direction is one of the few things she does for herself. We've covered a lot of ground over the last two years. I've watched her open up and relax her grip on life. Yet every so often we catch a glimpse together of some of her distorted views of God; remnants of her childhood's rigid faith tradition and her own penchant toward perfectionism.

During this particular session, she wanted to explore her lifelong and recently churning desire to write—something at the time she had little opportunity to indulge. As I asked her about her longing to write, she lit up, expressing strong desire and energy toward practicing her craft. I posed the simple question, "Meredith, what if this longing is from God? What if God is stirring this desire in you to write?"

She sighed, "That sounds too good to be true."

"Really? Why is that?" I posed.

"Well, life is just so full with taking care of the house, teaching preschool, and my role at church. It feels selfish to take time away to write."

I listened, wondering where the root of that idea came from. I decided to ask, "How do you think God views your gift of writing?"

"Well," Meredith began, "I suppose he's given me this gift and would want me to use it. I just have a hard time believing it's as important as my other responsibilities."

Then I asked, "Tell me how you feel when you write. How would you describe your experience of yourself when you're in the flow of writing?"

Her eyes welled up and she quickly responded with several strong words. "I feel alive. Excited. Creative. So happy and full!"

"And why would God not want that for you?" I mused.

Meredith's head dropped. She looked as though she was wrestling to admit the reason. And then she said, "I think I'm afraid that I enjoy writing *too* much. And if I enjoy it *too* much, God will take it from me because it competes with my devotion to him."

Stop for a minute and reflect on how you think Meredith is imagining God. What does her admission of fear suggest she believes about God, what God is like, and how God thinks and feels toward her?

Interestingly, this revelation surprised Meredith. She had no idea that she thought of God as a jealous and fickle gift giver. It didn't make sense in her head, but she knew it was what she feared in her heart. I suggested that she take time alone in prayer and process this revelation *with* God. "Tell him you're afraid he will take this away if you like it too much. Ask the Spirit to help you see and hear how God really feels about you and your love of writing. And listen to what the Spirit has to say." Meredith agreed to do so and share during our next session if anything transpired from the interaction.

RESPONDING TO A DISTORTED GOD IMAGE

Most of our distorted images of God portray God as hostile toward us in some way. Just as hostility in another human provokes defensiveness, so hostility on the face of God evokes our own self-protective responses. We generally will want to turn away from God, to hide our hearts, or to pretend to be okay because we're afraid of God's anger, disapproval, or retribution. Yet often this defensive turning away is so subtle, so unconscious, that we have no idea we're doing it. We quietly close our hearts or shift them ever so slightly away from the One we feel afraid of or fear disappointing.

The first step in healing a malformed image of God is to *become conscious* of it, to notice the feelings of fear or vague guilt or subtle avoidance this hostile God image evokes. Keep in mind: you can still go through the motions of praying, serving, or pretending to be spiritual—but you will feel self-protective toward God as you do. Prayer, the movement of opening and attending to God, is the central place you will notice that you've drifted from keeping company with the Spirit. You'll typically avoid praying or pray about everything that has nothing to do with what you're really feeling and fearing about God.

The second step, once you've noticed that you've turned away, is to *turn back*. And the only way to turn back is to do so from your heart in prayer. But this time your prayer must become real. It must be about how you truly think and feel about God or how you truly imagine God thinking and feeling toward you. You will need to wrestle, like Jacob and the angel, in a struggle with your god image and the real God. You will need to ask God questions, complain against God, curse, if necessary, and cry by all means. And you will need to lament. And somewhere in the midst of your struggling, you must ask Jesus to let you see his face, to show you who God really is.

During this tussle, what will hopefully become apparent is a clearer recognition of how your distorted image of God differs from God's true nature. In Meredith's case, she came to see the lie she believed: that God was threatened by her taking pleasure in something other than God. That god is stingy, selfish, and begrudges her the gifts he's given her. Meredith needed to see the lie clearly and name it plainly. Then, once she could do that, she was able to compare it with what she knew to be true of God's nature from Scripture and her own experience of God and bring this realization into prayer with God.

Healing our distorted images of God often takes a long time and frequently requires an intervention of sorts. In the following biblical example, Saul, who becomes the apostle Paul, has an encounter—or more accurately an intervention—with the resurrected Christ. Read the following narrative, told from Paul's point of view as he reflects on this experience.

Removing the Scotomas

Paul laid down his pen and stared out the window. The letter he was writing to the growing, yet unruly fellowship in Corinth was stirring up lots of emotions and memories. He paused and recalled his own journey to Jesus; it was widely different from theirs, yet his misperceptions of God were just as destructive. That decisive day was still fresh in his mind. God seemingly had branded it on his heart.

He remembered that morning as he was kneeling, reciting his well-worn prayers, and how he felt disrupted, uneasy, as if his sense of the straight and level horizon to which he oriented his sights was beginning to tilt. He had just returned from his latest crusade against the followers of Jesus. He had been there to watch that so-called believer Stephen pay with his life for his betrayal of the God of Israel. This ignorant man somehow spoke clearly, even convincingly of his God and courageously died for his faith, forgiving the men who stoned him. It was disturbing for Saul to recall how Stephen had looked directly in his eyes and repeated the very words that Jesus had uttered as he died: "Forgive them, Father, for they don't understand who they are harming or what they are doing."

Afterwards, in moments of solitude and prayer, he couldn't avoid thinking about the gnawing inconsistency between the righteous convictions he clung to and the devastation he was creating for these simple men and women who followed a deceased rabbi named Jesus. He heard their descriptions of himself: arrogant, cruel, unjust, unrelenting, mean-spirited, vindictive. How he regretted it now—his temperament well-suited to view God as mistrustful and miserly. He couldn't ignore his part in transposing some of his baser instincts onto God, but he also could see how his entire faith culture was enslaved to these distortions.

Then came the day he initiated a new campaign against the Way. About mid-morning as they rounded a small rise near their destination, Saul was suddenly thrown from his ride with an urgent, blinding light. Stunned, he lay on the ground, unable to see, his head and his body shaken and his sight blurred. As he rubbed his eyes and looked up, it was like he was seeing the world through a dense, impenetrable fog. Unable to see who was in the light, he did hear a direct, uncompromising voice say, "Saul, Saul, I've been watching you, and I've been experiencing the wrath that pours out of you in the name of your God. Why, friend, are you harassing me in these gentle, yet brave people? Can you tell me what fuels your hatred of us so?"

That was many years ago, and now he knew better what fueled his hatred. He now knew that at his core he wasn't vindictive or cruel. Like many, he'd been blinded by the god of this world and could only see its harsh black-and-white distortions. He closed his eyes and his heart quickly filled with gratitude as his eyes softened with tears. Now God, as well as everything and everyone else, looked so different. The *scotomas*—blind spots—in his mind and heart had been removed and he could see clearly God's heart of radical love.

After he had drifted for several minutes recollecting, he picked up his pen again and began to write from the deep well of his own experience. "God is patient; God is kind, doesn't boast; there's no arrogance in God." As he re-read what he'd written, he crossed out the word *God* and wrote the word *love*. For him now, there was no distinction. Aware that once he

would have passionately despised those he was writing, now
he had a father's irrepressible love and prayed that his words
would help these new brothers and sisters recover their sight
and see the beauty of God's true face and nature.

Let's be clear about what's at stake here—what it will cost us
and our relationship with God and our community if we live out
of a distorted God image. Instead of living mindfully in the present,
we will remain preoccupied with past failures and future strategies
to protect ourselves from God and seek to control our own destiny.
Instead of being real and authentic, we will betray our deepest
longings and live from our false-self identities. And instead of
being truly free, we will experience a life of idolatrous confinement,
shrinking into little people who serve a little god.

Unless and until we pay attention to what we know in our hearts
that is deeper than all the distortions and deceptions in our minds,
until we surrender to the ultimate Lover of our souls, we will be
bound to our functional god image, no matter what we say or sing.
Indeed, we need conversion! We need God to remove the scotomas
from our spiritual sight so that we can more and more embrace the
reality of Love's overwhelming love for us and all humankind.

Sit quietly in silence for several minutes. Then scan your memory and consider a specific time in the last few days or weeks when you were at your best. What are the primary feelings you experience as you consider God observing you?

Now, recall a time recently when you were not at your best. How do you imagine God's expression and feelings toward you?

Review the questions of both a healing and a harming God image. Choose a question that most accurately pinpoints your God image from each list. Reflect on your own story. When and how was this functional God image formed? What new insight do you have about how this way of seeing God has affected your relationship with God?

Once you identify a distorted projection, take time to name it clearly and specifically. How does it compare with what you know to be true of God (1) in Scripture, (2) from your tradition, (3) from your own experience of God, and (4) through reason? (See appendix 1, "A Word About Experience," which describes these four sources of spiritual insight and their relationship to one another.)

How will you seek to heal this image? What steps will you take? What must God do for this healing to happen?

CHAPTER 7

IMAGINING JESUS

*No one has ever seen God. But the unique One, who is himself
God, is near to the Father's heart. He has revealed God to us.*

JOHN 1:18

THE FIRST TIME WE ATTENDED A SERVICE at St. Paul's Episcopal Church in Indianapolis, we arrived early and found a seat
toward the middle of its magnificent sanctuary. Once the service
began, we clung to our programs like a map of a foreign country
we were visiting for the first time. It was a bit dizzying, all the
standing, kneeling, reciting, and responding. And then came time
for the dramatic moment in the liturgy for the Gospel reading. We
clutched our notes, head's buried, trying to follow the cues. When
we finally looked up, to our shock we discovered the entire congregation in front of us had turned around and were facing us!

We hadn't noticed that the priestly entourage had processed
from the chancel down the steps to the middle of the aisle, drama-
tizing the coming of Christ, God incarnate, who made his home
among us. We were stunned to discover all eyes on us, as we awk-
wardly made a half turn toward the aisle. As uncomfortable as this
was, the meaning of the procession wasn't lost on us. No one had

to explain it. We were deeply stirred by this vivid depiction of Christ coming into our midst.

This element in the Anglican and Episcopal liturgy poignantly symbolizes God drawing near to us through Christ, a movement packed with meaning. Yet because of the realities of being so earthbound and human, and the notion of God often seeming so remote and ethereal, the significance can evade us. It's no secret that we all struggle to experience the personal love of God, to imagine God actually pursuing us. Though identifying as believers, we tend to function as agnostics when it comes to trusting our experience of a loving, pursuing God within ordinary life.

In Ronald Rolheiser's book *The Shattered Lantern*, he writes, "We live in an age of unbelief. What sets us apart from past generations is that today this is as true within religious circles as outside them. The problem of faith is especially one of unbelief among believers." While we might be on the lookout for God, our experience of finding God and relating to God "as a living person to whom we actually talk, from whom we seek ultimate consolation and comfort, and to whom we relate person to person, friend to friend, lover to lover, child to parent" is really quite rare!

Both of us experience this difficulty, as do our directees. Sincere and earnest in seeking God, we still feel disappointed by our own doubts of God and lack of assurance in God's individual and particular love for us. What are we to do? Where do we turn for help to reignite faith that is not merely a moral code of ethics but a vital and engaged relationship with God who is near? We both have personally experienced and confirmed in our spiritual direction practice the value of turning toward the Gospels for assistance. Introducing the *Gospels as a lens*, or more precisely a telescope, often has been most helpful. Specifically, learning to engage the imagination as we prayerfully read a Gospel story is what enlarges and enlivens our awareness of Christ's presence and love for us.

A telescope brings near that which is far from us. It does so through the use of two lenses, an eyepiece lens and an objective lens. The lenses are convex in shape, bending the light toward us and causing what we're looking at to appear closer. If we use this as an analogy, we imagine the Gospels doing the same thing for us by magnifying Jesus. They bend the light toward us, helping to bring Jesus near in order to facilitate a vivid encounter with him. Rather than attempt to describe this kind of process, we'll illustrate it through an experience that David had as he engaged his imagination in a Gospel story and had a profound encounter with his brother Jesus.

I'LL BE YOUR BROTHER

One morning, as I (David) was coming to after my second cup of coffee, I returned to my reading of the Gospel of John. I, along with countless others through the ages, have found this particular Gospel and intimate portrayal of Jesus especially absorbing. At the time, I was considering making some big shifts vocationally and was feeling unusually alone, even vulnerable. Taking another sip of coffee, I opened to where I'd left off in John 7. Read along with me from *The Voice* translation of the Bible.

> After these events, *it was time for Jesus to move on*. He began a long walk through the Galilean countryside. He was purposefully avoiding Judea because of *the violent threats made against Him* by the Jews there who wanted to kill Him. *It was fall*, the time of year when the Jews celebrated the Festival of Booths.
>
> **Brothers of Jesus** *(to Jesus)*: Let's get out of here and go *south* to Judea so You can show Your disciples there what You are capable of doing. No one who seeks the public eye is content to work in secret. If You want to perform these signs, then step forward on the world's stage; *don't hide up here in the hills, Jesus*.

Jesus' own brothers were *speaking contemptuously*; they did not yet believe in Him, *just as the people in His hometown did not see Him as anything more than Joseph's son.*

Jesus: My time has not yet arrived; but for you My brothers, *by all means*, it is always the right time. *You have nothing to worry about because* the world doesn't hate you, but it despises Me because I am always exposing the dark evil in its works. Go on to the feast without Me; I am not going *right now* because My time is not yet at hand.

This conversation came to an *abrupt* end, and Jesus stayed in Galilee until His brothers were gone. Then He, too, went up to Jerusalem.

As I finished reading the story, I just sat for a few minutes. As I often do when reading a Gospel narrative, I relaxed, entering an internal posture of wordless prayer, and simply let the raw, unedited story play in my mind like a scene from a movie. I imagined Jesus, isolated as he traveled on back roads to avoid the religious vigilantes seeking to do him in. Walking in the shadows, he carefully made it to his back door and quietly slipped in.

There in the kitchen I imagined him finding his half-brothers huddled around the table eating some cold fish. The fire had mostly gone out and there was a mingled smell of smoldering coals and sweaty young men. As they looked up at him, Jesus felt conspicuous by his presence outside of the circle. No one scooted over to make room for him, they just stared. Finally, one brother broke the silence, his tone a voice of taunting. The accusing words hung in the air, and Jesus took a long, drawn out breath and sighed. Then in a cool manner, he simply told them the time wasn't right for him to return to Judea. Jesus intimates, though not too subtly, that he'd be relieved to see them go and leave him alone. And so, off they stormed, slamming the door behind them.

He hears their scornful laughter as they mutter some of their well-worn insults and walk away.

Transfixed by the scene playing out before me, I found myself whispering my own prayer. "Well, at least you *had* brothers. I didn't even get to experience the taunts and teasing of siblings." As an only child, I thought I'd put to rest decades ago what was normal for me, a life with no brothers or sisters. The muffled lament in my voice betrayed an unacknowledged desire.

As I sat with the jolting and disheartening exchange between Jesus and *his* brothers, I heard a clear, human-sounding voice in my imagination say, "I'll be your brother." Not completely trusting what I'd heard, I kept listening. Again, in clear, simple speech I sensed Jesus reaffirm what he'd just said; "David, I'll be your brother." I'd been earnestly seeking a deeper, more personal experience of God over the previous months; at times it seemed as if to no avail. And here I was, hearing Jesus volunteering to be my brother.

In this momentary exchange, I began to open my heart to what has become one of the greatest joys of my life: pressing deeply into the rich and earthy experience of having Jesus as my brother! I shared the experience with my spiritual director, and even today, a few years later, she occasionally will ask me, "And what would your brother, Jesus, have to say?" It all began with my simple willingness to enter into this story written two thousand years ago in a way so unpretentious a kindergartner could do it. Jesus tells us that to experience his kingdom we must become like little children. Could it be that in part it's their God-given imagination that we must recover if we are to have eyes that really see and ears that really hear the voice of this One so near?

BENDING THE LIGHT

While it is true that Western Christians have access to information about the Christian life more than ever before, it is all too obvious that this information hasn't translated into life change. We are no more Christlike, loving, compassionate, and selfless than previous generations of less-informed Christ-followers. Why is that? While there are numerous explanations, we'd like to highlight one relevant reason: *information alone will not change you.* In fact, hoarding more and more information can obscure or even shield you from an actual experience of God. Only when that information becomes fuel for the imagination are you changed at the deep level of your identity. It is through the imagination that you discover the port of entry where Christ wants to meet you and embrace you with his love and healing presence.

Imagination may not be what you think. It's not pretending or making something up that isn't true. Try this experiment: stop for a minute and picture someone you love. Try to picture that person vividly. Are you making that image up or are you simply calling to mind a representation of this person who is real and alive? In the same way, when you engage your imagination while reading a Gospel story, you are not making up what happened or what Jesus was like in the story. You are envisioning what happened in the story so it becomes real to you, so Jesus becomes real to you.

When you read the Gospels with imagination, here are some things to notice in order to recognize the place where his story and your story connect, where the Spirit is inviting you to be open to Jesus as Jesus draws near to you. The first thing to pay attention to is the way you are *provoked* by the story. Think back to David's experience. As he imagined Jesus relating to his brothers, he had an unexpected reaction of jealousy. "Well, at least you *had* brothers." Learn to notice those kinds of reactions, positive or negative, in how the story hits you.

Another element particularly important to identify is *how Jesus seems to you in his humanity*. The telescope of Christ's humanity often bends the light and pulls him more closely to you. You relate to Jesus as he relates to you. He becomes more real, more compassionate, and less remote. And if you believe Jesus "is himself God" and "is near to the Father's heart" and "has revealed God to us," then you also become more confident in your experiences of God in prayer and ordinary life. Those encounters match the Jesus you've met in the Gospels. For David, paying attention to the human-sounding voice of Jesus convinced him he was hearing correctly that Jesus wanted to be the brother he never had.

As you sink deeper into the encounter, pay attention to the story's *intersection* with your own story. As David lingered with the images of Jesus and his brothers, it eventually struck a nerve. He identified his own sadness in never having a brother, something he'd thought he'd long ago accepted about his life. This became the opening where David encountered Jesus. Distinguishing the intersection and naming it is an important moment in the process. Stay with this in prayer until you become confident that you know where this story touches you.

The last thing we suggest is to *be attentive to what you hear* with the ear of your heart. Jesus says that his sheep follow him because they know his voice (John 10:4). So listen for his voice, his words or message to you. Recall that David heard Jesus the first time he offered to be his brother but didn't trust what he heard. So he listened for his voice again. We encourage you to do the same. Listen, and when a thought comes to you, test what you hear. Does it sound like Jesus? Does it sound like something Jesus would say? Is the tone, as well as the meaning, consistent with the nature of God who is loving and life-affirming?

David described engaging his imagination with this story as the beginning of an experience that has been one of the greatest joys of his life: relating to Jesus as a brother. Remember that when you have similar encounters, perhaps more subtle or even more dramatic, this often represents the beginning of a shift in your relationship and intimacy with Christ. Keep pressing in, continue recalling the experience, stay with the passage for some time so that this port of entry stays open and you linger there with Jesus, the lover of your soul!

REENGAGING WITH JESUS

I (Beth) had been meeting with Ryan for about a year for spiritual direction. I always looked forward to my deep and thoughtful conversations with Ryan, a young Episcopal priest who had graduated from a nearby seminary. They flowed naturally, thoughtfully, with focus, and more than the usual amount of profanity. We laughed and cried together as we talked about his dreams and phobias, as well as the inhumane ordination process he was in the midst of.

When we started meeting, he divulged that he was more comfortable talking about his experience of God and the Spirit, but wasn't too sure where Jesus fit into his spiritual life these days. Ryan had been raised in the church and knew all the Gospel stories. For some reason they just seemed unhelpful as he considered the mysteries and tragedies of life. Having met with others who were in similar places, I assured him that it was fine with me and that he didn't need to put on his "I love Jesus" button for our meetings.

And so our sessions continued over the months until one day as our conversation unfolded Ryan shared, "I don't know what's happening, but I've fallen in love with Jesus again! I've been trying and trying to leave him in the past, but God has seemed very distant and remote recently. So, I started reading the Gospels and something's shifted. It's as if Jesus and I are in my small room together where I pray and we're having this wonderful, secretive time together. It still feels private, and I'm not sure I'm ready to make any big announcements. Yet it's been quite profound to feel this close to Jesus again."

As I listened to Ryan, I couldn't help but smile. I told him that as I experienced him today I sensed more energy and joy than before. He smiled and told me that as he reflected back, it was his pride, coupled with some tragedies he'd witnessed, that had created a wall of resistance to the all-too-human portrayal of Jesus—not to mention the mascot-like way many paraded him around. He'd thrown his lifelong friend out with the bath water and couldn't think his way back. "Somehow," he said, "Jesus didn't give up and just waited for me to find my way into his story again."

RESPONDING WITH IMAGINATION

Without a doubt, we owe a debt of gratitude for the encouragement to use our imagination to the sixteenth-century figure Ignatius of Loyola. His personal example combined with promoting the free use of our God-given imagination as a means of deepening our experience of God in prayer has been a pure gift. Ignatius, the founder of the Jesuit movement, recommends to us an approach to Scripture, and especially the Gospels, that makes full use of the powerful faculty of holy imagining.

To say it again, when we speak of imagination in this context, we are not referring to a world of make believe or fantasy, but rather another legitimate way of experiencing what we know in our heads. Do you believe God is the one who has given you the gift of imagination? Do you think God might want to use your imagination as another way of drawing you closer to his heart? Since God draws near through every other aspect of how you're created, why not through your imagination too? Of this form of prayer, James Martin (a Jesuit himself) says in his book *My Life with the Saints*, "Today this type of meditation is the primary way I encounter God in prayer."

So, when we speak of imaginative prayer, we are simply describing another way of prayer that makes active use of the imagination. In *The Ignatian Adventure*, Kevin O'Brien likens the approach to the creative act of visualizing an event as if you were making a movie.

When we lose ourselves in the scene of a film, we are aware of every detail; the vividness of sights, sounds, smells, colors, and emotions that draw us into an "as if we were there" experience. To quote Ignatius, the invitation is "to see with the sight of the imagination."

For some, using this magnifying lens in prayer and reading Scripture comes naturally. For others it requires a bit more explanation or initial steps to follow. Here are a few that we hope will be helpful.

Select a Gospel passage you are drawn to. It may be a favorite story or one you are curious about. Although this form of prayer can be entered into using any text, it is particularly well-suited for Gospel stories and is especially designed to help you encounter Jesus in the flesh as he moved among humanity in a real and unpretentious way during the first century.

Now read the passage several times. It can be helpful at some point to read it out loud and hear your own voice deliberately forming the sounds of the words. Become familiar with the story as you seek to be at home with it. Notice the setting, the characters, the situation. Who is the central character? What's the problem? What's the outcome? What's unusual?

Next, imagine that the event is happening right now. And rather than remain a detached observer, allow yourself to be *in* the story as an active participant. If you find this difficult, imagine describing the scene to a child by making it as vivid as possible.

Linger and fill out the scene as much as you can. Who else is there? What do they look like? What are they wearing?

What are the surroundings like? The sights, the smells, the tastes? What's the weather like? What's the mood of the place?

Where am I standing? What am I wearing? How am I feeling?

It may help to also envision *being* one of the characters. Who am I? What am I noticing from this person's vantage point?

Where is Jesus? What is he doing? What does his expression look like?

Listen inwardly to what God is drawing your attention to.

Talk to the characters in the scene if you'd like, especially to Jesus. Speak from your heart. What do you want to say or ask? Now listen to what is said in response.

Return to the present moment, while continuing to be open to God. Is there anything else you want to say or ask? Remain still and ask if there's anything else God wants to say or offer you.

While imaginative prayer isn't the only or even the highest form of prayer, it is a tried-and-true approach, one that has greatly assisted men and women for centuries. Envision having the desire to see deeper into the Milky Way and being offered the gift of a powerful telescope. Can you imagine (there's that word again!) the gift-giver standing next to you as you step up to the lens, tilt it upward, and see for the first time what you've longed to see all your life? That's the gift we've been given within this capacity called imagination.

If you've never encountered Jesus through the prayerful use of imagination, we'd like to invite you to look through a Gospel story for a few minutes much like you would look through a telescope to bring what seems distant near.

Read the following story from Mark 9:33-37 a number of times and familiarize yourself with its details.

> At last, they came to Capernaum where they gathered in a house.
>
> **Jesus:** What was it I heard you arguing about along the way?
>
> They *looked down at the floor and* wouldn't answer, for they had been arguing among themselves about who was the greatest *of Jesus' disciples.* He sat down with the twelve to teach them.
>
> **Jesus:** Whoever wants to be first must be last, and *whoever wants to be the greatest* must be the servant of all.
>
> He then called forward a child, set the child in the middle of them, and took the child in His arms.
>
> **Jesus:** Whoever welcomes a child like this in My name welcomes Me; and whoever welcomes Me is welcoming not Me, but the One who sent Me. (*The Voice*)

Pick a character you are drawn to and want to identify with or possibly one you are reluctant toward and resist. Where are you standing or seated? What are you wearing, and how are you feeling? Look around. Who else do you notice? What's the space around you like—the sights, sounds, smells, atmosphere?

Notice where Jesus is. How does he seem to you? What's his expression like? What's he doing?

Now listen inwardly. What emotion is this scene stirring in you? What do you want to say to Jesus? What do you want to ask?

Wait for Jesus to respond. As you imagine Jesus being with you now, what does he say in response to what you've just experienced?

Finally, rest in the present moment as you straddle the experience of the first-century Jesus, the Jesus of your imagination, and the mystical and living presence of Jesus who is with you now, in *this* time and *this place*.

CHAPTER 8

EXPECTATIONS
AND ASSUMPTIONS

Therefore, we who have fled to him for refuge can have
great confidence as we hold to the hope that lies before us.
This hope is a strong and trustworthy anchor for our souls.

HEBREWS 6:18-19

WE'RE OFTEN UNAWARE OF our expectations until life doesn't
measure up to them. That was my (David's) observation as I listened
over Skype to Ron lament how disappointed he was with God and
his many unanswered prayers. For a few years now, Ron and his wife
had been pursuing international adoption. Like so many cases, they
were dragged through an inefficient and maddening process because
of the adoptive country's corrupt and dysfunctional government.

Believing God had asked them to take these steps, and believing
that what they wanted for this particular child was for his good, they
tenaciously worked the angles—unsuccessfully. One disappointment
after another after another had begun a not-so-subtle demolition
of Ron's faith in God's providence. He came to me angry, bewildered, with his heels dug in. The God of his current understanding
had let him down, and Ron resented being disillusioned.

As I listened to Ron grieve the loss of his definitive assumptions of how God *should* act within the circumstances of his life and through his fervent prayers, I recognized my own familiar refrain along with countless others who've begun to question their expectations of God. While chapter six was about God's *presence* and what God's nature is like, this chapter focuses on God's *actions*, how God actually works to influence change in our lives and our world.

Each of us will have to confront, sooner or later, and probably more than once, our understanding of how God accomplishes his divine will, in particular the idea of what it means to us that God is in control. Does it mean that God strong-arms us? Or that God passively allows everything that happens to happen? Does God have only some influence over what happens but more importantly is present to us in whatever happens? *How do you currently think about God's influence or control in your life and in the world at large?*

As we press into these questions, often through a similar crisis as Ron's, it can start a deconstruction process in which we begin to disassemble some of our restrictive ways of thinking about God's operations in the world. While this can feel destabilizing, in reality it has the potential to be a profound moment of rebirth, an extending of the tent pegs that allows more room for God to be God.

When your expectations and assumptions are being tested during the storms of life, it helps to relate to them as a *floating anchor*. Like sailors in a storm, we put down a floating anchor to steady us. A floating anchor is designed to prevent the ship's capsizing from the winds and waves when all other maneuvers are no longer possible. Rather than casting down a fixed anchor, a floating anchor causes the ship to slow down (not stop) and turn toward the storm surge (not crosswise or backward).

If your expectations and assumptions of God are not fixed and immovable but rather are beliefs that you hold firmly yet fluidly, dynamically and responsively, this attitude will create sufficient space for God to work within the givens of life. You will still have a secure anchor to hold on to but will avoid the trap of being stuck in naive patterns of belief that sabotage your relationship with God and could cause your faith to capsize. "Therefore, we who have fled to him for refuge can have great confidence as we hold to the hope that lies before us. This hope is a strong and trustworthy anchor for our souls" (Hebrews 6:18-19).

CONFRONTING OUR ASSUMPTIONS
AND EXPECTATIONS

We all have certain assumptions about and expectations of God. Many of them are unconscious, like an operating system on a computer, humming along and keeping things going until . . . until something happens that you can't account for, something that doesn't make sense to you as you know and understand God. Your suppositions about God's ways of being toward you and in your world collide with a difficult situation, an experience of suffering, an irresolvable conflict, and you are bewildered! Your initial recognition of this collision between your expectations of God and the reality of your life come through the jolt of disappointment with God.

The first time we recall one of these storms of life where we confronted our assumptions of God was early in our marriage. To our surprise and delight, Beth became pregnant. From the initial symptoms, and in the weeks that followed, the viability of the pregnancy was in question. After several ultrasounds, it was confirmed that the embryo was no longer alive. A blighted ovum, the doctor called it.

The ovum wasn't the only thing blighted. Our faith and confidence in God were as well. In our young and naive perspective as sincere followers of Jesus, we assumed that if we did our best to be faithful, God would hold up his end of the bargain. If we worked hard to live for Jesus, then he would protect us from any arbitrary, senseless loss. As inexperienced and unsuspecting as we were, God was inviting us to "put an end to childish ways." It was time to stop working the formula we believed would ensure that we got what we wanted from God and open ourselves to the reality of life with God.

When life collides with your beliefs and you experience the jolt of disappointment with God, pay attention to your *reaction* to feeling disappointed. It's such a hard thing to admit to ourselves or someone else, let alone to God. Is it okay to feel disappointed with God? Will God be angry with me or pull away from me if I admit that I'm disappointed? It's difficult to reconcile the way life actually is with who you thought God to be. In this precarious situation you might have any number of reactions.

One reaction might be to *overspiritualize* your situation in an attempt to shield God from getting a bad rap. "Well, God knows the reasons." Or "I know that everything that happens is sifted through the hands of God." It's not that these statements don't have some validity, but if you're too quick to offer these explanations, they may be an effort to assuage your disillusionment and protect yourself from being out of sorts with God, not to mention protecting God's reputation.

Another reaction is more subtle. You *suppress* your disappointment and anger by ignoring it. You sweep it under the proverbial rug and keep going. The thought of engaging your disappointment with God is too overwhelming and complicated, so you power on! More than likely, however, you begin to move along a trajectory that is slightly off-kilter from God. After all, who wants to cozy up to a God who is undependable? A God who doesn't make sense? One who could have done something and didn't—or did something and shouldn't have? And so your heart for God grows cold and you begin to drift with barely a notice.

Or you can just *be mad* at God and dig your heels in, as Ron initially did. You can hunker down in your anger and resist letting go of your inflexible ideas of how God should be. You can camp out in your resentment that God's ways aren't the way you want things to be.

Each reaction above has its own challenges. And each reaction has only one way out: you must slow down and turn toward the storm, your floating anchor in tow. Listen in as David continues his spiritual direction session with Ron and see what happens when he faces this storm head-on, yet with a slower, more contemplative attitude.

SLOWING DOWN AND FACING THE STORM

"Ron, I certainly hear how very disappointed you are in God and confused by these blocked goals you had to adopt your son. Are you able to speak with God honestly about your disappointment?" David asked.

Ron shifted his body away from the screen for a minute and heaved a deep sigh. "Yes. I feel like that's all I've been doing—all I've been praying about. I just can't get beyond my anger and frustration with God at asking us to pursue this adoption—let alone all that we've gone through to try—and then him doing nothing to make it happen!" Ron snapped.

"Ron, what if God is just as disappointed—just as angry and frustrated as you are?"

Ron looked at me a little bewildered and shrugged. "How could God be? Isn't God the one who's in control and has the power to move mountains?"

"So, do you think that God always gets God's way? Does God always get what God wants?" David inquired.

Ron stumbled for a moment. "No. I suppose not. I can't look at the way things are in the world and believe that."

"So, again, what if God is just as disappointed and angered by all this as you are? What if God is brokenhearted with you and for you and your son? How does that affect you?" David asked.

Ron was still for a moment, appearing to search his own heart and awareness, and then replied, "Well, I guess it makes me feel less alone. . . . I still wish God would break through all the corruption and red tape and bring our son home! Yet if I imagine God feeling disappointed *with* me, I'm definitely more willing to be open to him."

"Ron, what if for a few moments you sat with the image of Jesus being angry and upset with the situation along with you and see what happens. Are you willing to try that now?" David asked.

Ron said sure, he'd be willing to try. He sat for probably three or four minutes. I watched his countenance and body language as he settled in and then seemed to relax a little more. Then finally Ron looked up.

I asked him, "How would you describe your awareness of Jesus now?"

He spoke slowly and with measured words. "Jesus seems kind and compassionate and caring. I imagined him sitting close to me, leaning toward me to support me, and I feel his empathy. . . . It's like we both know how hard it's been, and we're just here, together in the silence, for each other."

"What's that like for you, Ron?" David queried.

"It's really good. It's calming. It's a place to begin again, to start rebuilding our relationship and trust," Ron concluded.

THE LAW OF RETRIBUTION

Many biblical narratives provide a window into similar stories like Ron's and our own; people who were surprised that life took the turn it did and shocked that God didn't intervene as they assumed God would. And sometimes in the story, from our vantage point as the reader, we can see the clouds parting as the characters recognize their misplaced expectations and open to God who is always motivated by love and the greater good. There may be no better illustration of this than the story of Job. A wealthy and prosperous man who was praised by God as blameless, upright, God-fearing, and evil-shunning—it would appear that Job had the formula down.

And a lot of good it did him. Unbeknownst to Job, he became the linchpin in a dynamic dual between Satan and God (Job 1–2). In round one, Job experienced a series of calamities that destroyed all of his livestock and killed all of his children. In round two, Job experienced a painful, horrific health crisis that nearly took his life. Less apparent in this narrative is an unspoken and underlying assumption running throughout and likely the author's point in telling the story.

In the ancient world, people were heavily invested in the "law of retribution." The law, simply stated, goes like this: people get what they deserve. If you do good things, you will be rewarded by the gods. If you do bad things, you will be punished by them. *Yet Job's story defies that assumption.* He's the guy who's blameless, upright, fears God, and shuns evil. And look what happened to him.

For forty some chapters, Job thrashes about in a sea of confusion, in the chaos of his own faith crisis. He questions God, argues with God, and defends himself to God and his three dubious friends. And then, finally, after what seems like an eternity of silence, God speaks, addresses Job, and asks him a series of questions, including:

- "Where were you when I laid the foundations of the earth?"

- "Have you ever commanded the morning to appear and caused the dawn to rise in the east?"

- "Who makes the rain fall on barren land, in a desert where no one lives?"

- "Can you direct the movement of the stars—binding the cluster of the Pleiades or loosening the cords of Orion?"

When God had finished his cross-examination, Job becomes quiet. Very quiet. Then after some time, he responds.

> I know that you can do anything,
>   and no one can stop you.
> You asked, "Who is this that questions my wisdom with
>   such ignorance?"
>   It is I—and I was talking about things I knew
>   nothing about,
>   things far too wonderful for me.
> You said, "Listen and I will speak!
>   I have some questions for you,
>   and you must answer them."
> I had only heard about you before,
>   but now I have seen you with my own eyes.
> I take back everything I said,
>   and I sit in dust and ashes to show my repentance.
>   (Job 42:2-6)

The guy who had been praised as blameless, upright, god-fearing, and evil-shunning finally realizes, "I had only heard about you before, but *now* I have seen you with my own eyes." That's often the sensation we have once we consent to see God and reality through a larger, less-confining, less predictable framework. We experience what feels like conversion, a rebirth of our faith and sense of God. It's as though we never really knew God as we once thought we did. And the only appropriate response to the God we now see is to be quiet.

THE FLIP SIDE: EXPECTING TOO LITTLE

While the examples we've focused on are primarily about expecting too much from God, or more accurately, having fixed and inflexible expectations of God, there's a flip side to our unconscious lenses of expectations and assumptions. Sometimes we expect *too little*. Sometimes our assumptions of God are so anemic and blasé that we expect nothing, and so we look for nothing. Having no expectancy of God prevents us from opening our eyes to the presence of God all around us.

During our spiritual direction training course, we do an exercise with our students in which we create a list of theological assumptions related to spiritual direction. These are the assumptions we have about God and God's way of relating to us that form the bedrock of the spiritual direction practice. Together, we name the things we expect of God that enable us to offer spiritual direction and participate with God in the work God is doing within a directee's heart and life.

For instance, the assumption that God wants to be known and communicates with us is always on the list. We assume that God takes initiative to speak and reveal his love and true nature to us. We believe that God desires friendship with us. That God is not withholding but is generous and self-disclosing. If this wasn't the case, then spiritual direction would be pointless. Because these are our assumptions of God, they help inform what to look for as we scan the horizon of our internal and external landscape. If we don't believe this is the case, then we will fail to look for or notice revelations of God within our ordinary lives, as well as within the lives of our directees. Fitting expectations awaken us to the Spirit's movement in and all around us.

RESPONDING TO WHAT THE STORM DREDGES UP

These destabilizing storms will likely happen more than once as you persevere along the arduous path of faith. Rather than brace yourself against the storms or dig your heels in, your best tact is to become curious about what the storm dredges up in this clash between your circumstances and your current beliefs, assumptions, and expectations of God. Yes, storms can be terrifying! Yet God in his good and loving desires for you wants you to grow up and become a fully functioning adult in the way you live and relate to him. God's supreme desire is for you to fully know him and the way he works.

Here are four responses that we have found to be grounding during these kinds of experiences. Consider them as the means through which you create a floating anchor for your assumptions and expectations of God.

Determine to seek God with all your heart. If there's one over-arching promise in Scripture that is unequivocal, it's that when we seek God we will find God if we search for God with all of our hearts (Jeremiah 29:13-14). When your belief systems can no longer contain what has happened in reality and you are in anguish because God isn't who you thought God was, the temptation is to turn from God in your anger and disappointment. Don't do it! Instead, turn toward God, determined to seek God with all your heart until you find God.

Vent your true feelings in prayer. If you determine to seek an audience with God, by all means come clean with him. Tell God how you feel, why you're disappointed, what you don't understand. Learn to vent your feelings in prayer. Nothing revives your prayer life more than becoming honest with God and telling it like it is to God. That being said, supplement your lamenting with listening. Look God square in the face and explain yourself. And then get quiet, like Job, and notice your awareness of God—how God seems to you as you come to God raw and naked.

Question your assumptions and expectations. When life and beliefs collide, it's an important time to take a long, hard look at the God of your current understanding. Who is this God? Is it the God of your youth? The God handed down to you from your tradition? What about this God could be a false projection? Be willing to question your assumptions and expectations that belong to the

God of your previous understanding. Are you being invited to enlarge or relax the parameters you've put around God?

Loosen your attachments. Once you begin to question your belief system, you will be invited to loosen your attachments to your assumptions and expectations. This is a time to release God from being a certain way, answering prayers exactly as you'd like or always making sense to you. At the same time, you are invited to trust that whoever God is and however God does God's work in your life, God is good and motivated by love.

Open up to the mystery who is God. Once you've identified the false narrative you've been living by, the formula you were working to get God on your side, let go of your childish ways. Open up to the mystery who is God. Give some slack to your anchor and let it float. Allow God to expand the parameters of your understanding and soften the edges of your expectations so that you can embrace more of who God truly is. When asked for the divine name, God told Moses, "I AM WHO I AM" or "I WILL BE WHO I WILL BE." Will you let God be the great I AM?

Take some time and ask God to show you your own assumptions or expectations concerning the movement and action of the Spirit in your life and world.

Some essential areas to consider might include

- how God shows personal concern for and is involved in the details of your life

- how God communicates to you in specific ways and forms

- how you interpret God's inaction or silence in areas of life that matter greatly to you

- how you experience God's prevailing and persistent love toward you

- how much freedom God has to be who God is and act as a free Agent

Write your thoughts in response to the prompt:

I say I believe that God is _____ but I more often expect God's attitudes or actions to be _____.

- Which of my own assumptions and expectations about God have I allowed God to adjust?

- Which ones may need to be further examined as I become open to the possibility of their limitations?

- How might these expectations and assumptions ultimately prevent me from being receptive to God's free and particular love for me?

CHAPTER 9

THE HOLY FLAME

*Didn't our hearts burn within us as he talked with us
on the road and explained the Scriptures to us?*

LUKE 24:32

IMAGINE YOURSELF IN Emmaus around AD 33.

This has to be the longest seven miles I've ever walked, I thought to myself. I've traveled the road to Emmaus countless times during my thirty-seven years, but today my body feels every weary step it takes. My nephew Cleopas is lost in his thoughts at the moment. As hard as the last several days have been for me, it's not the first time that my hope has been dashed. But for him, I've feared that this could be the blow that slays his young, untested faith. I'm exhausted from all the discussions we've been having, yet we both keep trying to make sense of the senseless.

Who's that coming up behind us? I wonder, catching the strong cadence of another's steps. I know there have been thieves along this stretch, so I turn quickly to confront this stranger. *He doesn't look dangerous*, I think to myself, suddenly relieved and glad for the interruption.

"Can I join you?" the stranger asks. "It looks like we're headed in the same direction." I nod and Cleopas moves to make room in between us.

"I've been following you for the last mile or so, and by the looks of your gestures and raised voices it seems you've been having quite the discussion. Tell me what's gotten you so stirred up," the man inquires.

Cleopas stops dead still in the road and just looks at him, staring. "You must be the only living soul within this whole region who doesn't know what happened in Jerusalem this weekend."

"Really? Well, tell me. What happened?" queried the stranger.

My nephew is still worked up and launches into his version of the events that have left both of us confused and broken. He gives a lengthy account of our relationship with Jesus of Nazareth, our hopes that Jesus was the Christ, and how those hopes have been dashed. Out of breath and blurry-eyed, Cleopas finishes with the strange reports from other disciples of Jesus' missing body and encounters with heavenly messengers.

The stranger is now shaking his head as he looks at my face and then at my nephew's. "What's the matter with you, you simple, simple men," he mutters. I feel my blood start to boil. Who is this stranger who thinks he can interrupt our grief and then insult us? Before I can tell him off, he continues. He seems patient again, sharing with Cleopas and me his take on both the events of recent days and how they were implied throughout our Holy Scriptures. His explanations are so absorbing, novel in a way, that the miles seem to speed by as he mines the prophets' holy words for connections and meanings I've never considered before.

Cleopas interrupts the stranger as we enter town. "At last—we're home!" The man stops and bows slightly to us, then turns to continue walking. "Please, good sir," I blurt out. "Be our guest. It's getting too late to be out on the road alone." Seeming as if he had nowhere more important to be, he accepts and follows us. We sit by the fire while my wife prepares a simple meal for us. I keep studying this stranger as he dozes in the chair next to me. He stirs as my wife calls us for dinner.

I typically give thanks, but by some inner prompting I ask if the stranger would offer our prayer. His hands, so callused and scarred, reach for the freshly baked bread. He lifts it to heaven, breaks it, and gives it to me and my family. Then a surreal thing happens; something hard to describe. It's like time freezes for several seconds and then suddenly my eyes open. "It's Jesus!" And as soon as the words come out of my mouth, I look at Cleopas and then back to where the Stranger was sitting, and he's gone!

Stillness falls on the room. The young children are gaping at the empty chair and then at Cleopas and me. "How could we have been so slow to recognize him?" I say to my nephew, as well as to myself. "Didn't you feel it when we were with him, talking on the road? It felt like a holy flame warming the inside of me as I listened and he offered his deep insights. It was him, wasn't it? He was with us and he was opening our eyes to his reality with every word he spoke."

A HOLY FLAME OR A COOLING EMBER?

How long has it been since you had an experience with Jesus like the one described in Luke 24? Not a physical encounter or theophany, but an emotional and spiritual encounter as Jesus spoke to you through some words of Scripture? If you are like many who come to us for spiritual direction, it may have been a long time. Instead of a holy flame, your experience may feel more like a cooling ember when it comes to your engagement with Scripture. That's how it had been for Stacey, one of Beth's directees.

Stacey and her husband had been deeply entrenched in a dynamic, evangelistic, and authoritarian church. After two decades of involvement and several wake-up calls to the parental nature of the leadership, she and her husband had enough and left. Though this happened more than a dozen years ago, the power this unhealthy church exercised over them still wreaks havoc in Stacey's thoughts, motivations, and relationship with God. And it certainly has gummed up her ability to hear from God through the Bible.

One day, during a spiritual direction session, Stacey apologetically confided in me (Beth) that she couldn't read the Bible any more. She felt bad. Really bad. And very guilty. And yet every time she tried to read or even listen to a sermon, she either glazed over or felt triggered by what she read or what was said.

"Stacey, how do you imagine God reacting to your difficulty with the Bible?" I asked.

She looked away, closed her eyes, wrinkled up her nose, and then said, "I imagine him being very disappointed with me and upset that I can't get over this!"

"Do you think he understands why you struggle? Do you think he feels, maybe, compassion or sadness because he longs for you to come to him unhindered?" I asked.

"Yes, I can believe that," Stacey replied. "I know he does understand. It's just that the Bible used to be so important to me and so meaningful. When I'd read it, I really did feel the presence of the Holy Spirit. It helped me hear from God. I miss that."

At this point, I took a little time and shared briefly my own journey with church wounds, the Bible, and recovering my soul. I recalled the morning I was in my home office praying, lamenting to God how I'd felt robbed of my relationship with Scripture because I'd experienced so many self-righteous, heavy-handed Christians using it as a weapon to defend their positions and get their way. I finally cried out in exasperation, "I have the right to my own relationship with Scripture and I'm not going to let them steal it from me!" That was a real turning point for me.

After I shared my story, I talked with Stacey about a different way of coming to Scripture, one that is less about getting answers from the Bible and more about opening up to God through the Bible. I introduced Stacey to a spiritual practice called lectio divina, which we'll explain to you shortly. But before we do, let's consider how to recognize different approaches to Scripture reading and how each affects the way we respond to the Spirit within the texts of Scripture.

ADJUSTING OUR SCRIPTURAL LENSES

At one time or another, each of us was told that the Bible is a unique and privileged book through which God seeks to communicate truths that are important for us to know. Whether we grew up hearing stories of Noah and the ark, Jonah and the whale, David and Goliath, and Jesus walking on the water, or later as adults discovered this massive survey of Israel and early Christianity's attempt to make sense of their identity and experience of God, eventually we found ourselves face-to-face with the notion that these words written by human authors could still be carriers of the divine voice. We also learned, and are likely still learning, that our posture toward Scripture can either draw us deeper into a true experience with the lover and keeper of our hearts or further away because of unhealed wounds.

For many of us, this journey with God and the Bible has been like our marriage vows, for better or for worse. We've had to learn and then unlearn ways that Scripture was misused to support a human agenda and—as if starting over—relearn a more prayerful way of approaching this sacred text in order to hear God whispering through it again. For some, God's voice is as clear as it was when we were first given these sacred books and letters. It's important to cultivate a generous heart toward one another and remember that we each have a unique journey with God, and we each have a unique relationship with Scripture. Wherever we find ourselves as we traverse the valleys and mountains of our personal experience, we cannot escape this enduring question: How do I engage with these ancient words in a meaningful and growing way in order to keep attuned to God's heart toward me and my neighbor?

The earliest teachers of the Christian Bible, the church fathers, were deeply aware that its words were filled with mystery. They, along with countless others throughout history, recognized the Bible's depth of richness that goes beyond what the human authors could have known or foreseen. These human authors wrote of "a country" they were looking forward to, a country they could call their own (Hebrews 11:13-14). This fuller sense is often referred to as *sensus plenior*.

This perspective in no way minimizes the value of rigorous study that helps illuminate the author's point of view as well as the cultural, literary, and linguistic issues that are vital to reading these books in their historical context. In fact, much misreading of difficult passages can be cleared up when cultural context is acknowledged. However, as Michael Casey reminds us in his book *Sacred Reading*, "The revealing work of the Holy Spirit did not cease with the drying of the ink on the last page of the Book of the Revelation. Inspiration, properly speaking, is the guidance given to that complex of activities that resulted in the *writing* of the biblical books. The Spirit is also active, however, in the *reading* of Scripture."

THE FOUR APPROACHES TO SCRIPTURE

In some Christian traditions, in particular evangelicalism, followers are taught that there is only one way to read Scripture. This dominant perspective views the literal-historical sense of Scripture as the prime, if not exclusive, approach to reading and responding to these ancient words and stories. What is ignored, to our impoverishment, is that the people of God for centuries, both before and after the Enlightenment, have embraced multiple approaches to Scripture concurrently. We'd like to introduce four approaches that can enlarge our all-too-often constricted attitude toward how the living Word speaks through the written words of Scripture.

First, as already introduced, is *the literal and historical reading* of Scripture. With this method you, along with the assistance of biblical scholars, seek to discern what is often referred to as authorial intent. What was the human author of this book, this teaching, this story seeking to convey to the audience? Your understanding of the story of God and God's people in Scripture is greatly enhanced as you understand the historical context and culture as well as the type of literary genre of the particular text you are reading.

The second approach can be described as the *Christological* or *allegorical reading.* Martin Luther described the Bible as "the cradle of Christ." As the early disciples sought to make sense of their firsthand encounters with Jesus, they frequently turned to the Old Testament and began to see prophetic symbolism, allegory, and echoes of the living Christ. It was as if Scripture became stereophonic, increasing and deepening their faith in Jesus the Messiah. When you engage Scripture through this lens, you are listening for ways the text amplifies or supports the Jesus you know from the Gospels: his nature, his gospel, and his teachings. One extremely significant effect of this approach is that we begin to develop an image of God that is more like Christ.

The third approach is generally referred to as *moral* or *behavioral reading.* At first, this sounds legalistic and pragmatic, as though you simply take the ethical or behavioral commands of Scripture and put them into practice. Yet that is not the emphasis in this approach. The focus here, to use a popular term, is on your *formation.* Its focus is on how the Spirit employs Scripture to transform you from an image carrier to a living likeness of God on earth. Whatever other value there might be in Scripture, it can quickly devolve into a mere "clanging cymbal" if the visible effect is not one of becoming more like Jesus.

Finally, we come to what is best called the *mystical reading* of Scripture. Here the written Word becomes a sacrament of the living Word, offering Christ's presence as bread to nourish your hungry souls. In this way of engaging Scripture, Christ personally addresses you through the written Word, and you are awakened to your true self, your deeper longings, your need for love, and the satisfaction of your desires. This is where your faith and your experience become juicy again. And through this mystical encounter with the risen Christ, carried by these sacred words, your heart is warmed toward God and softened toward others.

Can you see what's at stake in order to sustain our seeking and encountering God through the medium of Scripture? Simply reading the Bible in its literal-historical sense would be like studying a topographical map of the Rockies and telling yourself you've climbed all of its fifty-four fourteeners. Prayerfully weaving your way through Scripture with all these approaches in hand awakens the heart as well as the mind and will.

RESPONDING: HOW SCRIPTURE BECOMES PRAYER

It has been one of the great rediscoveries of our times to experience the resurgence of interest and practice in Scripture reading known as lectio divina. The phrase is from Latin; *lectio* simply means "reading" and *divina* means "sacred" or "divine." I (David) discovered this ancient practice after three years of seminary and becoming absolutely burned out on the Bible! So much tedium had been spent on the historical-critical method of reading Scripture that my soul felt shriveled, I was spiritually drained of life and in desperate need of a reprieve from the intensity. (Truth be told, for a season, the only thing I read was Louis L'Amour westerns.)

Finally, after a few years, I began reading Scripture again, but this time along the lines of lectio divina. And then something happened that hadn't in a long time. I began to encounter the living Word with the same tone of voice as I had as an eighteen year old reading the stories of Jesus for the first time. Was this a return to my first love, as John described it in Revelation 2:4?

This approach to sacred reading of a brief passage of Scripture is neither a technique nor a prescription. Rather it's an internal posture of engaging with the living Word in the written word as we seek to "listen with the ear of our heart." It gently leads us to respond authentically to God, who is addressing us through this sacred text.

Briefly, in its classic form, lectio divina has four movements. Each movement is introduced by a single Latin word.

Lectio (reading). In this movement you simply read the Scripture and gather in the facts as you notice them. Your prayer might be that of Samuel's: "Speak, your servant is listening." As you listen or read the words, you pay attention to the word or phrase that stands out and seems to speak uniquely to you. You may find yourself curious about the word or phrase, drawn in as if that particular word or phrase lifts from the page or even shimmers to you.

Meditatio (meditate). In this movement you open yourself to be addressed more personally. You read the Scripture again and let Jesus speak to you. You rest on the word or phrase you've chosen and slowly absorb it, noticing where it intersects with your own life right now or what its message might be suggesting to you. A simple question to ask is, "God, what do you want to say to me?" Or "God, what in me needs to hear this word from you?"

Oratio (prayer). This third time, you read or listen to the Scripture passage again, slowly and thoughtfully. You seek to let your heart open and yourself respond to God. Assuming that you have had a growing sense of God speaking to you, what do you want to say to God? How do you want to respond to Christ's words to you? Trust the Spirit as you become emotionally involved and share with God, as with a friend, whatever is being stirred in you.

Contemplatio (contemplation). You read the Scripture a final time. By this time, you should be familiar with its rhythms, its repetitions, and its drama. Simply receive the words as if your heart is rich, fertile soil in which a Gardener is lovingly placing a seed. This movement corresponds well with the mystical sense mentioned previously. Contemplation is the room where you simply are invited to *be*: to be with God, to be yourself, to be loved and in love. Simply surrender to God's presence and seek to rest in union with God beyond concepts, feelings, or any particular actions.

STRIKING FLINT

Let's pick up with Stacey, my (Beth's) directee, as she experienced lectio divina for the first time. Recall that Stacey had expressed difficulty with reading Scripture. It often seemed irrelevant or she felt angst from something she read. Recovering an open and receptive attitude toward the Bible can take a long time, and it's likely that even if we do, we will still be triggered by simplistic, reductionistic interpretations.

"So, Stacey, how about if I lead you through a lectio divina and see what it's like for you to listen to Scripture through a different approach? What do you say?" I asked.

Stacey was more than willing to give it a try.

I prayed a silent, earnest prayer, *Lord, help me. Bring to mind a passage that would be meaningful for Stacey.* We sat in silence for a couple of minutes. The theme of acceptance kept coming to me and then the story of Jesus and the young ruler in Mark 10:17-21.

"Okay. I think I know what passage I want to read." I turned to it in my Bible, and before I read the passage I asked Stacey to listen attentively for the word or phrase that stood out to her. I encouraged her not to censor what she noticed but to speak it out once I finished.

As Jesus was starting out on his way to Jerusalem, a man came running up to him, knelt down, and asked, "Good Teacher, what must I do to inherit eternal life?"

"Why do you call me good?" Jesus asked. "Only God is truly good. But to answer your question, you know the commandments: 'You must not murder. You must not commit adultery. You must not steal. You must not testify falsely. You must not cheat anyone. Honor your father and mother.'"

"Teacher," the man replied, "I've obeyed all these commandments since I was young."

Looking at the man, Jesus felt genuine love for him. "There is still one thing you haven't done," he told him. "Go and sell all your possessions and give the money to the poor, and you will have treasure in heaven. Then come, follow me."

When I finished, Stacey paused, looked a little uncertain, and said, "I don't know why, but the phrase that stood out was 'since I was young.' That seems kind of strange."

"That's okay. Don't worry about it. We'll see if it becomes clear as to why." I responded. Before I read the passage a second time, I suggested that Stacey keep pressing into the phrase "since I was young" as she listened, and then ask herself, *Where does this phrase connect with my life right now? What in me needs to hear this phrase?*

I read the passage again, slowly and meditatively. Stacey sat in silence for a few minutes. She appeared quiet and captivated. Finally, she broke the silence and said, "I feel like Jesus is reminding me of our history together. I've known him 'since I was young.' He's been faithful to me and has never given up on me." She seemed to relax a bit as her confidence that she could hear from God grew.

I nodded, smiled, and suggested that she listen a third time and reflect on how she desires to respond to what Jesus is saying. "Ask yourself what prayer is forming in me? Is there something I want to say or do to respond to Jesus?"

I read the passage a third time and we sat for several minutes in silence. I saw Stacey shift her body a few times, as though she was wrestling a bit. I could tell she was concentrating, listening deeply to her own heart as she listened to God's heart for her. Finally, when she spoke up, she explained more of what "since I was young" has come to mean over the process of this meditation.

She recognized Jesus affirming her history with him. She also reflected on how she related to Jesus when she was young. She was bold and certain and ready to change the world. She told him she didn't feel that way anymore and sensed Jesus being okay with that. She realized that her youthful zeal didn't have the deep roots she thought it had. And she felt like Jesus was inviting her to trust him to help her learn how to be with him now, in this place, at this stage of her life.

I read the passage one final time and invited Stacey to sit with it, with Jesus, perhaps imagining him looking at her the way he looked with genuine love at this young man. She did, and then I ended our time with prayer, aware and grateful for the holy flame of love that lit up Stacey's face.

Being on the lookout for God in Scripture is an invitation to read differently. We could even say to read without aim, without agenda, to read slowly, leisurely, and prayerfully. One way you can practice reading differently is to write the passage you are contemplating in an open, free-form layout. When text is dense and print is small, we tend to read quickly. When you create white space and limit the amount of text on a line, you are inviting pauses, reflection, lingering. Prayerfully read this portion of Psalm 63:6-8 from the *Benedictine Daily Prayer* using some of the prompts of lectio divina below.

> On my bed
>
> I remember
>
> you.
>
> On you
>
> I muse
>
> through the night.
>
> For you
>
> have been
>
> my help.
>
> In the shadow of
>
> your wings
>
> I rejoice.
>
> My soul
>
> clings
>
> to you;
>
> your right hand
>
> holds me fast.

Notice what words or phrases you are drawn to again and again. Ask the Lord what might be God's invitation to you in those words. Listen and be still. As you wait patiently, what is gently coming to mind?

What do you want to say in response? What questions for God are coming to mind? Enter into a listening-responding dialogue for a few minutes. Be bold and don't be overly concerned about getting it right. You'll recognize when your thoughts are obscuring what God wants to say to you. Don't be surprised over time if your thoughts and God's thoughts have a similar quality. We take on the vernacular of those we love.

Is God inviting a response of some kind on your part? If so, consider your willingness to surrender in love. Or maybe God is offering you simply the deep gift of his companionship. Rest in the present moment and be here and nowhere else.

If you feel you'd like to write a few thoughts to help you remember what this experience with God was like, how you felt and what he is saying to you, briefly record what comes to mind.

CHAPTER 10

GOD'S BIG BOOK

Then the LORD God planted a garden in Eden
in the east, and there he placed the man he had made.

GENESIS 2:8

"WELL, HOW WAS YOUR TRIP?" I (Beth) asked, once Ruth had
settled into her chair in my office. She let out a long, deep, lovely
sigh and responded, "M-a-g-nificent!" This mid-winter trip to
Santa Fe has become a yearly pilgrimage for Ruth, a senior pastor
of a local church, which has been a challenging role for her. While
her denomination has ordained female clergy for some time, her
experience within her congregation, as well as her denomination,
has often felt like swimming upstream against a turbulent,
downstream current.

So, for Ruth's own health and well-being, she began a practice
a few years ago that "Come mid-winter," she would leave family
and work behind and head to a place where no one knows her,
where she can detach from all her responsibilities and be with God
in nature. Ghost Ranch and the mountains surrounding Santa Fe,
New Mexico, have become an ideal place for her to heal from some
of the bumps and bruises sustained while pastoring a local church.

While Ruth's experience of pastoring is not uncommon among the female clergy we offer spiritual direction to, what is unique is Ruth's acknowledgment of her need for renewal and her commitment to seek renewal through immersion in the natural world. As she began this rhythm of returning to Santa Fe each year, she discovered something profound happening: her soul was being repaired. This trip has now become essential for the sustainability of her life and calling as a pastor. But what does nature do for Ruth? What do we need that is so uniquely met within the realm of God's creation?

While undoubtedly there are numerous ways to respond to these questions, perhaps the most profound answer is that nature immerses us in an environment where everything lives from its true essence. *Nothing in nature is a façade.* A rock is a rock, a blue jay is a blue jay, a creek is a creek, and a wild flower is a wild flower. And that's significant because we—like no other living thing—struggle to be real and to live from our true essence. Only human beings become confused about who we really are.

When we enter the solace of nature, we are enveloped by a world that exudes integrity. Each living thing vibrates reality, unwittingly drawing us toward wholeness and true being. The sum of creation and all its parts transmits authenticity, groundedness, and peace, which heals us and restores our souls. That's what the psalmist David is intimating as he describes the habits of the Lord, his Shepherd:

> He makes me lie down in green pastures;
> he leads me beside still waters;
>   he restores my soul. (Psalm 23:2-3 NRSV)

The healing and repairing effect of this experience can't be underestimated! And there's just no other domain like it in our human existence. In this chapter, we will consider how nature can become a healing balm in our inundated lives and a conscious lens through which we look for God and form a deeper connection with God through engagement with the created world. We'll begin by sharing a bit of our own personal history with nature as a place of God encounter.

ORIGINAL ENCOUNTERS

In our early years neither of us was raised within a faith community nor did we receive any conventional religious instruction. However, it's been a source of joy and mutual fascination to compare our initial brushes with a felt presence of God during childhood. We both recall in the most vivid ways our sense of being held, immersed, and seen by God while exploring the wonders of creation.

Lacking (and not really needing) the language of faith, Beth recalls her childhood home on an acre plot that backed up to a tree-lined creek. Meandering along its banks, she watched tadpoles, dragonflies, and schools of minnows, and recalls the startle of an occasional water snake. She spent her days exploring this world where she felt most at home with herself, and it became a channel through which she began to perceive its Creator.

David was given a larger plot of nature to explore at his grandparents' home, affectionately named Clear Lake. In southern Indiana, with forty acres of dense woods and rolling hills and ravines, as well as a five-acre lake, he discovered the gifts of solitude and freedom to roam, listening to the wind in the trees, cracking open geodes, and falling asleep in the sun by a welcoming stream. He began to develop a deep, contemplative inner life as his awareness of God ripened in this boyhood paradise.

As we look back over six decades now, neither of us feels the least bit cheated by not having received any explicit, early religious instruction. In fact, we feel extremely grateful to have been given the gift of a direct experience of God through God's wild and wondrous creation. These were our earliest moments of genuine spiritual awakening. We think the Celtic Christian tradition says it well: the Bible is God's little book and creation is God's big book! Thank God that we are immersed in a world crammed with the divine, equally accessible to the young who have yet to learn to read and the old who are weary of an all-too-worded existence.

THE WORLD OF MANUFACTURED THINGS

Within the Judeo-Christian creation narrative, our original dwelling with God was a garden filled with all the wonders of creation: rivers, trees, varieties of vegetation, and creatures of all sorts. Compare that with the setting in which you currently live out your days. From the moment you wake, from your first trip to the bathroom and kitchen, and then on to work, you're relentlessly bombarded by manufactured things rather than God-created things. The assault continues when you return home. It follows you through the door into your personal spaces where you exercise, relax, and tuck yourself into bed at night. What's most disconcerting is that this bombardment barely registers on your consciousness. And so goes another day of complete preoc-cupation in the world of humanly created things.

Minute by minute during your waking hours you're confronted by the essential and trivial marvels of manufacturing, including up to twenty thousand advertisements flashed by your wearied eyes every day, telling you what you don't have and where you are defi-cient. The net result of your modern, crowded living condition is that there's very little clear space left in your head or heart for your own thoughts, let alone thoughtful thoughts and interactions with God. These kinds of contemplative impulses have been pushed to the margins of your sight lines, seeming to exist only as a wavering mirage in your peripheral vision.

Most of us cannot, nor would we want to, opt out of human civilization and live completely off the grid. Yet at times we desperately need relief. The age-old spiritual practice of fasting is increasingly relevant to our incapacity for mind-clearing, contemplative pause. And it's not just food that we need to forgo to reset our spiritual priorities. We need regular fasts from many things, but perhaps most of all we need regular fasts from the human-made world. We need to fast in order to cleanse the toxins accrued from overconsumption of stuff and disengagement from our true selves. We need a break so we can hear ourselves think.

Just as clear sunlight reveals how dirty our windows are and how much they need to be cleaned, nature cleanses the windows of our minds and senses, helping us notice and attend to the churning waves inside us that distract us from our real lives, lives that exist as pure gift. In the vast, expansive realm of the natural world, we confront our own small, relentless self-absorption. The wilderness creates space to move from egoic thinking to deeper reflection on important life questions and to notice and respond to our sense of God's vast presence and personal revelations to us.

Consider a few of these possible reflections that may open up when encircled by nature's care:

- What is it like for me to be surrounded by life that has no need of me?

- Who am I when I'm not needed?

- Surrounded by so much abundance and gratuitous provision, how can I live a more trusting existence?

- What do I really need or want that might reestablish my sense of well-being and equilibrium?

Nature, indeed, has innate healing properties that help you become more clear-minded and less self-absorbed. Its integrity beckons you to reconnect with your truest self and orient toward God and the deep joy of your calling. Soaking in the beauty of the natural world can make you sane again.

In Scripture, nature is prolifically referenced as a balm for worn minds and souls. And never is it more profoundly illustrated than in the story of King Saul, a man beset with mental illness and whose one remedy came via the psalms of nature, written by someone deeply acquainted with nature—David the shepherd boy.

Read the following story, told from the perspective of Saul's son Jonathan as he observes the way nature's songs calm and clear his father's troubled mind and spirit.

Psalms of Nature

Jonathan had grown up with his father's dark moods and had learned early to carefully read the atmosphere at home. As a young man himself now, he appreciated the strain his father carried as Israel's first king. There was continual pressure to keep up with neighboring nations and to remain true to Israel's God-given identity. Tonight, King Saul was profoundly out of sorts, almost as if tormented by forces beyond his own brokenness and the burden he bore.

Jonathan's best friend was the paradoxical young man David, a brave warrior, natural singer-songwriter, and a passionate lover of God. Jonathan's father often compared Jonathan unfavorably to David, but Jonathan had nothing but genuine respect and brotherly affection for him. David's musical compositions had an earthy yet heavenly quality: prayer songs he simply called psalms. They came from the heart and spoke to the heart, soothing the mind and inclining one's trust toward God. Jonathan's father, Saul, had often benefited from David's gift, and when in a troubled mood Saul would compel David to play to bring some relief. In Jonathan's words:

David came as soon as I sent for him and again sang for my father, who was in one of his disturbed states. The king eventually fell asleep to David's voice and poetic images, sleeping soundly for the first time in days. David's songs stayed with me too, the images lifting not only my father's demented spirit but my own depressed spirit, as well.

The heavens declare the glory of the Creator;
    the firmament proclaims the Handiwork of Love.
Day to day speech pours forth
    And night to night knowledge is revealed.
There is no speech, nor are there words;
    Their voice is not heard; yet their music resounds through all
        the earth,
    And their words echo to the ends of the world.

"How do you do it, friend?" I ask David.
    "Do what?" he replies.
    "Where did these beautiful images and melodies
        come from?"

Taking his time, as if reliving many past and private moments, David began to speak. "As you know, I was the runt of my family. So I was assigned the task of watching sheep while all my brothers were given grown men's work to do. At first I was resentful and would just sling stones to keep myself busy. But the longer I was out in the wilderness and took in the morning skies and overflowing brooks and eagles and the blooms of the desert, something came alive in me. It was as if the very earth and sky had a voice and was singing, singing to God and of God. What's more, I found myself humming along. Lines would just come to me.

    You bring me to green pastures for rest and lead me beside
        still waters.
    Those who walk with God are like trees planted by streams of
        water that yield fruit in due season and their leaves flourish,
        and in all they do they give life.

How glorious is your dwelling place, O Blessed Architect of
the universe! Even the sparrow finds a home and the swal-
low a resting place.

You watered hardened souls, filled with stone and weeds,
softening them with kindness and blessing their growth.

"As I listened, the music of the desert found a deeper place in
me, and I started to weave my own tunes into these prayer
songs. I can't believe I'm saying this, but I miss those long,
lonely days . . .

"Jonathan, I'm grateful that your father is helped by the music.
I know he believes it's my voice and my harp playing that
soothes him, but I suspect it's something else. You see, he's also
a man of nature, and yet he's so trapped by the burden of being
king that all he sees and hears are the pressures of humankind
and the threats of other nations. Whether he realizes it or not,
my songs remind him of the God he knew as a boy. They're an
echo of the One who created everything and cares for it all; the
Architect of the Universe who is immense and faithful."

As David and I walked together out into the night sky, I looked
up at the heavens, a million stars twinkling, and I understood
what he meant. I sighed a long sigh, opening my heart to the cos-
mos and noticing a quiet reassurance of its Creator's nearness.

A PRIVILEGED PLACE

We who live immersed in a world that is engineered and manufactured by smart technology can scarcely imagine an existence this
simple, this undomesticated, as David described. Yet don't you notice
within yourself the echo of desire to return to your original dwelling
where you might encounter God and be healed? Consider this
question posed by authors William Barry and William Connolly:
"Are there any privileged places or privileged events to which we can
go to put ourselves more explicitly in God's way?" Isn't that a

wonderful question? And the answer is *yes*! We, along with Barry and Connolly, believe that nature is unquestionably one of those places!

Aware of it or not, excursions into the natural world are an important ingredient in the spiritual diet of anyone sincerely desiring a more explicit experience of God. However, once you're there, what do you do? How do you recognize God through the conscious lens of nature? How do you connect with God and respond to God's invitation to return home to your true essence as you commune with God in the world he created? How does nature assist your faith becoming sight?

Let's return to Psalm 19, the psalm of David quoted previously, as a prompt to help us "put ourselves more explicitly in God's way" in nature and seek to recognize God's presence and action there. Read the following verses, slowly and thoughtfully, three or four times.

> The heavens declare the glory of the Creator;
>> the firmament proclaims the Handiwork of Love.
> Day to day speech pours forth
>> And night to night knowledge is revealed.
> There is no speech, nor are there words;
>> Their voice is not heard; yet their music resounds through
>>> all the earth,
>> And their words echo to the ends of the world.
>> (Psalm 19:1-4, *Psalms for Praying*)

The first thing that David suggests you do is to *look for the glory*. "The heavens declare the glory of the Creator." Have you ever looked up into the night sky studded with shimmering stars and marveled at the immensity and wonder of it all? That sensation of marvel or wonder or awe is your awareness of God's glory. *Glory* is such a difficult word to define or describe, but you know it when you see it. And you predictably see it when you look up to the heavens and see billowing white clouds pinned against the most gorgeous blue-of-all-blues backdrop, complete with shafts of light radiating from the sun. How does it not take your breath away? How does it not display that of God who is beyond you? How do you recognize God in nature? By noticing glory.

David also recommends that you *pay attention to God's handiwork*. And it is on display throughout the natural world! Have you ever studied the details of a wildflower long enough to notice its intricacies? Or the wings of a butterfly, the texture of a tree trunk, the geometric patterns on the back of a beetle? Each and every creature within God's world displays amazing design, artistry, and beauty! Take time to notice the bark on a sycamore tree or the veins of color in an outcrop of rock; stand at a distance and marvel at God's creative expertise.

David urges you to *listen for the wordless, soundless message within nature*. When you take in the integrity of nature and open yourself to what you sense and see, you often hear its message to you. It's not one that is detected audibly, yet it speaks like an eternal fountain of wisdom, ever available to those who press their ear to the ground. Listen! Is the authenticity of nature helping you identify where you need to repair, where you need to become real and whole?

RESPONDING TO NATURE'S REVELATIONS

Once you place yourself explicitly in God's way in the natural world and begin to recognize God addressing you, how do you reflect on and respond to these revelations?

Here is a gentle process to follow:

First and foremost, it's critical to simply *be* in this organic setting, experiencing it with all of your senses. Abandon any agenda for getting something from the experience or trying to make something of what you're seeing. Instead, just take it all in. Relax into it.

Let your mind go. Resist pushing your thoughts toward anything in particular.

Next, allow the whole landscape to touch you. Feel it through your skin's sensory receptors. Experience yourself as part of the whole. What is it like to feel your smallness in contrast to the wild and wondrous expanse of your Father's world?

Now pay attention to how this landscape speaks to you of God. What inaudible message does it express about God? How does God seem to you in this place?

How do you want to respond? What would feel like the most genuine response of your body, with your words, or in an unspoken, inexpressible prayer?

Respond directly to God in whatever way feels most genuine. Listen with the ear of your heart for God's response to you.

The rumblings of nature often generate a felt sense that God is in this place and he is holding it all together. This "big book" of God speaks with power and authority to both our physical and spiritual eyes. The apostle Paul says as much: "For ever since the world was created, people have seen the earth and sky. Through everything God made, they can clearly see his invisible qualities—his eternal power and divine nature. So they have no excuse for not knowing God" (Romans 1:20).

- Think back to your childhood and your relationship with the natural world. What was it like for you? How did you feel when in nature? Were specific places meaningful or magical to you? Reflecting back as an adult, do you have any vivid experiences you can name as moments of encountering God? What are they?

- Many of us have cultivated the habit of reading the Bible (God's little book) and praying each day. Consider intentionally spending a portion of each day for thirty days reading God's big book by getting out into creation (your backyard, a favorite park, a nearby river). This will take a little forethought and planning, but the experiment will be worth it. During your times in nature, consider praying in a similar fashion to lectio divina:

- First, notice what you are most drawn to. Don't overthink it.

- What is it prompting you to think about? What does it touch in you? What feelings, questions, associations, or needs from your own life come to mind?

- What prayer is forming within you? Express this directly to God. Talk with God about it.

- How is God speaking to you through what you've noticed? What do you sense God saying or leading you to become aware of as you contemplate whatever you are noticing?

- Finally, be still. Allow words of gratitude or trust to rise within you. Is there anything else you'd like to say to God? What is it? Is there anything else you're aware that you need from God? Name it.

Part Three

LOOKING WITHIN:
ENTERING THE
DEEP WATERS OF
YOUR SOUL

*Deep within us all there is an amazing inner sanctuary
of the soul, a holy space, a Divine Center, a speaking
Voice, to which we may continuously return.*

THOMAS KELLEY

CHAPTER 11

(DIS)ORIENTATION

"Get up and go to the great city of Nineveh. Announce my judgment
against it because I have seen how wicked its people are."
But Jonah got up and went in the opposite
direction to get away from the LORD.

JONAH 1:2-3

IMAGINE IF JONAH had a journal.

A few months ago, I was praying and seeking God, and in the midst of the silence I heard Yahweh speak to my spirit and urge me to go to that awful city Nineveh. I'd heard stories of what a worldly, wicked place it is. Immediately, I felt small, anxious, and deeply disturbed by what God was asking of me.

So like my name, which means "dove," I flew in the opposite direction. I did what seemed the only sensible thing to do. I set sail on a ship away from Nineveh toward Tarshish. I'm not sure whether it was the cool breezes, the warm sunshine, or the relief of taking control of the situation, but once I was on board I fell asleep like a baby!

This calm state, however, came quickly to an end. Soon a dangerous storm was upon us, causing even the seasoned sailors to want to run for their lives. Only problem, there was no place to run. After the sailors prayed to their gods and cast lots to determine who had angered the gods, I was chosen. It became obvious to everyone, including me, that I had brought this tempest upon us. I was running from my God, from my life, my integrity, and my duties. So, not being a particularly brave man, I asked the sailors to throw me into the sea rather than make me jump myself.

I'm not exactly sure what happened after that. I was battered about, losing consciousness, and in a dream-like state. I'm still convinced that I was swallowed by a giant fish as surely as I was swallowed by the sea. After some days, as if by some force of God, I was propelled from the belly of darkness onto the very shore I was seeking to avoid. Nineveh!

I should have been relieved to be alive, to have been rescued by some miracle of nature. But here I was, reluctantly consenting to deliver God's warning to these awful people, hoping against hope that God would annihilate them instead. I conveyed the warning: "You've got forty days to repent." And guess what happened? They listened and turned from their wickedness!

The forty days came and went, and the people of Nineveh were spared. I knew this would happen because I know how soft God can be, but it was a revolting offense to me! So here I am, finally coming to terms with my anger and hardness of heart in the face of God's generous love and forgiveness. I feel so far from God right now and completely disoriented!

What a mess Jonah made for himself! If only he'd been better practiced at paying attention to his interior life, he might have realized how far adrift he was from God. If we were his spiritual directors, we would invite Jonah to notice his deeper feelings, especially toward the Ninevites and toward God, who called him to go to them. We would encourage him to reflect on his beliefs, prejudices, and any experiences that fueled his hatred or fear. We would ask Jonah to notice the quality of the energy that drove him to board the ship to Tarshish and turn away from God. And likely we would introduce Jonah to the Ignatian concepts of *consolation* and *desolation*. Knowing experientially what they mean might have awakened him sooner to the reality of his spiritual orientation!

We've briefly introduced you to Ignatius of Loyola and how he recommended using imagination in reflecting on a Gospel story. Now we'd like to highlight a pair of interior lenses he identified as valuable in making sense of God's movement in our lives and our current spiritual orientation. Classically, the lenses of consolation and desolation are a means of discerning the interior posture of our heart toward God's presence and action. Unlike external or objective points of reference, they are internal and affective. When we notice what's happening inside us and compare what we find to the characteristics of consolation and desolation, we are better able to stay in touch with our soul's true bearings.

Following are some descriptions. See if they sound familiar to you.

When you experience consolation, you generally feel at peace, energetic, and joyful. You're full of gratitude—alive to your true desires and feel connected to God and others. When you experience desolation, you typically feel anxious, restless, fearful, and alienated from others. You are often plagued by feelings of insecurity and mistrust.

When you experience consolation, your thoughts are calm, centered, and originate from a true, wise, knowing place within you. When you experience desolation, your thoughts are often spinning, looping, and frenetic. You tend to catastrophize, believing the worst will happen.

When you experience consolation, you have the sensation that you are being *drawn* by the Spirit; there is healthy energy within you toward the invitations and path of God. When you experience desolation, you have the interior sensation of being *driven*.

The energy fueling your thoughts, attitudes, and actions often feels impatient, forced, and obsessive, *even if it is aimed toward holy ambitions and righteous causes.*

To be clear, what's being described is not simply feeling good or feeling bad. This chapter's focus is on *looking within* for signs of spiritual consolation and desolation that identify your stance toward God, toward God's invitations and movement in your heart. It's possible to sit quietly by a lake in a beautiful setting and feel a deep peace. While not dissimilar to the experience of spiritual consolation, this may or may not reflect our orientation toward God. Conversely, we could be deeply disappointed and upset about a bad health report and yet experience God's comfort and be completely oriented toward God in prayer and trust.

INDICATORS OF YOUR ORIENTATION

The spiritual journey is largely a matter of orientation. Is my life oriented toward or away from God? While that question may sound simple and straightforward, how do you discern the answer? Is it as clear as it sounds? You probably know that it's not. Or, maybe more accurately, not always.

There are three sources within your interior life that reveal your orientation toward God or disorientation from God: (1) emotions and feelings, (2) thinking and commentary, and (3) energy and drives. Each of these human capacities provides important information that can tell you whether you are experiencing consolation or desolation. Your challenge is to better understand what they are saying to you. Let's begin with the wild and wooly world of emotions and feelings.

EMOTIONS AND FEELINGS

"You shouldn't feel that way" was a regular refrain of my (Beth) growing up years. I got the impression that my mom related to certain feelings much like the arcade game Whack-a-Mole, and I should do the same. When an undesirable feeling like anger, disappointment, or mistrust rose up within me, I was to whack it on the head and send it back where it came from.

If you've grown up with this version of relating to certain emotions, banning certain feelings because you were taught they were bad, don't underestimate how this affects the depth of your relationship with God and everyone else in your life! Some of the most important sources of information at your disposal come from the realm of your emotions, information that is unavailable to you when you disown or avoid your feelings. This information helps you notice your response to God and deepen your intimacy with God and others.

Emotions and *feelings* are words we use interchangeably, but they actually mean something different. Emotions are instinctual and are produced by our primitive brain—that part of the brain that causes us to fight, flee, or freeze when facing potential danger. Emotions register in the body before we are aware of them; we've become adept at ignoring their signals. Feelings, on the other hand, involve interpretation of our emotions. In this case, a more sophisticated part of our brain adds content, memory, association, and meaning to the emotions we experience. While our feelings interpret our emotions, that doesn't mean they do so truthfully or accurately.

So, how can attending to your feelings help you be on the lookout for God? As mentioned earlier, you will typically feel certain sensations when you're in consolation or desolation. It's important not to label these as good or bad feelings. *All feelings are neutral. No feeling is a sin.* They are, however, important messengers that can alert you to how you are responding to God's timely biddings.

In consolation, you feel what might be described as right or harmonious feelings; your heart is lifted toward God, filled with gratitude and love for life. You feel and exude peace, joy, and patience toward self, others, and God. It's important to note, however, that consolation can also include less-idyllic feelings, like being scared or feeling grief over a loss, or the trepidation of choosing something that is difficult. These feelings are real and genuine but don't consume you. You feel them *and* the consolation that you are responsive to God and oriented toward your "true north."

In desolation, you feel what might be described as "off" or dissonant feelings. You feel tension and conflict, as though you're going against or away from your true self and God. Often the feelings of disorientation, agitation, and irritation accompany bouts of desolation. Again, it is important to note that you can experience certain forms of relief while in desolation. If you suspect that God is asking you to do something or go somewhere you don't want to go—as in the case of Jonah—you may feel relief on the surface of things. Deep down, however, your spirit is telling a different story. That story's plotline tells you that your true self, who knows and desires God, feels disregarded and homesick for God.

NOTICING SUBTLE AND SURPRISING EMOTIONS

As you can see, paying attention to your feelings and emotions is critical to discerning your orientation toward or away from God. Let me (Beth) provide an illustration through a session with one of my directees. Curt has been a campus pastor at a small Christian college for a number of years. Recently, because of a decline in student enrollment, the college eliminated his position. Curt was devastated! He truly loved his role and felt overwhelmed with disappointment. Simultaneously he felt a curious sense of relief and liberation. Let's pick up in the spiritual direction session after Curt told me what happened and we began to explore God's companioning presence in the midst of this unexpected turn of events.

Beth   I hear you feeling real grief and sadness over this loss. I know you loved the students and your colleagues and the role you had in their lives. Is there anything else you notice feeling?

Curt   Well, strangely, I also feel a hint of relief, as though I've been liberated. I can't say that I was aware of feeling trapped, but you know how hard it's been for me with all the anxiety over finances and budget. And of course I've talked often about my angst with the narrow theology and conservative political culture on campus.

Beth   Does this sensation of relief and liberation feel more like consolation or desolation?

Curt   Hmm. I know that I've had moments of desolation, especially when I let my anger over their decision get the best of me. I've even felt a few twinges of shame too. You know me—"I am what I do," and that's why I fear failure so much. But the relief and freedom I feel … it seems more like consolation.

Beth   How so? How is it different from the other feelings you described belonging to desolation?

Curt   When I sit with the relief I feel, I notice hope rising within me. I find myself dreaming about what my future might be like. I have all kinds of ideas, and some of them really do excite me. In those moments, I feel confident and energetic. I am able to trust that God is with me and hasn't abandoned me.

Beth That's interesting isn't it, that when you allow yourself to savor the freedom and relief, it sparks a host of other emotions that nurture trust in God. That sounds like God's movement drawing you into consolation, doesn't it?

    (*Silence*)

Beth Curt, as you sit with this experience of trust and hope *in* God, how would you describe your awareness of God?

Curt (*Pause*) I feel like God is with me in the assurance I feel—that even though I didn't see this coming, he's not taken by surprise. I sense God's closeness and experience him in the creative energy stirring inside me. I feel like he's for me and that we're working together toward what's next.

Do you see how paying attention to Curt's full gamut of emotions, especially the subtle and surprising ones, helped him recognize his spiritual orientation and experience of God? Though the realm of your emotions can often be intimidating and overwhelming to attend to, there is a wealth of valuable, even critical, information your emotions provide. Remember—feelings make terrible masters but important messengers!

THINKING AND COMMENTARY

Many who write about the interior life confirm that it's quite difficult, maybe impossible, to separate our feelings from our thoughts; they have a symbiotic relationship. To illustrate, let's say you're in a social setting with a group of people you don't know when someone tells a joke you're not sure you get. Suddenly, out of the blue, you feel the fear of embarrassment. It registers in your body and your brain scrambles, making associations with the emotion and adding gasoline to the fire.

Your thoughts and commentary come to the rescue, reminding you of similar times when you didn't get a joke and said something stupid! Now you feel even more agitated and awkward.

This happens to all of us. It's part of the mystery *and* misery of being human. So, how can you look within, pay attention to your thoughts and commentary, and learn what they have to say about your stance toward God? Again, identifying the quality of your thoughts in consolation compared to the quality of your thoughts in desolation is most helpful.

In consolation your thoughts will be calm and unhurried: creative, hope-filled, and open. Think of Curt's response when he savored the feeling of freedom and began to think about all the possibilities before him. In desolation your thoughts are often anxious and unbidden, compulsive and frenetic. They whip you up into a frenzy and keep you locked in their orbit. Curt spoke about his fear of failure and how he got caught up in it a time or two, yet was present enough to notice that old tape playing: "You are what you do. So you better not screw up!"

As Martin Laird writes, "It is precisely this noisy, chaotic mind that keeps us ignorant of the deeper reality of God as the ground of our being." Noticing and reflecting on the quality and content of your thinking and commentary helps you move from myopic ignorance to expanded awareness of God as your center of gravity. But doing so takes practice!

You simply begin by first noticing the quality of your thoughts. Is my thinking composed, or is it scattered and obsessive? Is it coming from a deep knowledge within myself or is it vain, superficial, and unproductive? Once you recognize the quality of your thoughts, in prayer you can ask God to help you discern the value of the content. Is this true or is it a lie? Is the Holy Spirit speaking to me or are these my old tapes playing again? This, friends, is the ongoing, interior work that transforms life into prayer and prayer into life.

ENERGY AND DRIVES

For some of you, you don't initially process life through your emotions or your thinking. What registers in your consciousness is more visceral and physical. You would describe it as an instinct or drive similar to the force and energy of a powerful river flowing through a channel. When something disruptive happens to you or around you, this uncontrollable force takes over before you have time to think or feel. When unchecked or unrestrained, your reactions can tragically become careless and destructive, like a river overflowing its banks. As you pay attention to the feedback your interior energy and drives provide, you will also begin to discern the alignment of your heart with or away from God, in step or out of step with the Spirit.

It's your energy and drives that prompt the useful question, Is my experience right now one of being *drawn* or *driven*? Both words denote bodily sensations more than pure feelings or thoughts. When you are in consolation, you have the sense of being drawn by the Spirit as though carried or assisted by a force not completely your own. You are living in the flow of life and of your true self. Life still requires effort, but it isn't forced or willful effort. When you are in desolation, however, you have the sensation of being driven, either by your own ego or from deeply ingrained reflexes. The energy of your effort, in this case, is compulsive, forceful, and impatient. Life becomes a task to master and a problem to solve!

Margaret Silf puts it this way: "The action of God on our lives is always, at its heart, experienced as a drawing. If we are feeling driven, then the prompting that gives rise to it is not from God but from the force fields of our own (or other people's) kingdoms." Becoming conscious of your energy and drives, both as they are happening and after the fact, is a reliable way to get in touch with the direction you're facing—toward God or away from God and

toward your own kingdom. If you want to live with your eyes open
to God's presence, you obviously need to be awake and frequently
consider your orientation toward God.

Reflect on this excerpt of Curt's story and notice where you
think he's describing the effect of his energy and drives on his
orientation. What words in his following comments belong to this
inner quality?

> When I sit with the relief I feel, I notice hope rising within
> me. I find myself dreaming about what my future might be
> like. I have all kinds of ideas and some of them really do excite
> me. In those moments, I feel confident and energetic. I am
> able to trust that God is with me and hasn't abandoned me.

The word *relief* is both a feeling word and one that describes
a bodily sensation. He speaks of dreaming about his future, a
comment that conveys a relaxed, contemplative state of being.
When he says that some of the ideas excite him, and in those moments he feels confident and energetic, all these words can be attributed to the quality of his energy and drives as he considers
what's next. Helping Curt notice his energy and drives reassures
him that he is in consolation; he is facing the right direction in
order to wholeheartedly respond to the presence and action of God.

RESPONDING TO (DIS)ORIENTATION

Attending to the interior life of your emotions and feelings, thinking
and commentary, energy and drives is essential if you are to wake up
to yourself and to God! And it is the ongoing work of your spiritual
life if you want to mature. There's no better way to learn to respond
to disorientation and orientation than through the spiritual practice
called the prayer of examen or examen of consciousness (another gift
from St. Ignatius). We will introduce this classic prayer to you by
inviting you to reflect over a period of time, a day or a few hours, and

look for experiences of consolation and desolation. You will need a journal and pen or pencil.

Begin by acknowledging God's presence with you right now. Ask Christ to companion you as you review your day.

Reflect over the last day or last several hours, reviewing each activity, conversation, or event as it unfolded. Remember how you felt, what you were thinking about, and how you experienced the energy in your body.

When did you feel alive, joyful, and at peace—thoughtful and calm, as though being drawn by the Spirit toward God?

When did you feel tired, nervous, or anxious—distracted or out of sync, as though drifting from God and driven toward your own agenda?

Noting what was going on at the time, write down when you experienced consolation and when you experienced desolation.

Go through the list of moments in consolation. Contemplate how you experienced God drawing you into consolation during that time, and thank God for the sweetness of his presence and attraction. Savor the memory of consolation.

Go through the list of moments in desolation. As you review them, do not scold or berate yourself for drifting from God. Contemplate how you got off track, wandered from God or resisted God's pursuit of you.

Choose the moment of desolation that seems most important to bring into prayer. Begin a conversation with God, asking for God's wisdom, insight, forgiveness, and grace.

As we suggested before, the quality of our spiritual life and journey is largely a matter of orientation. Is my life oriented toward God or away from God? Learning the qualities associated with consolation and desolation through practicing the examen is an invaluable means by which you can attune to your trajectory and ensure that you are on a path toward living a with-God life.

As you consider the three sources of information that indicate your spiritual orientation, which one is your go-to feature that helps you know if you are on track—emotions and feelings, thoughts and commentary, or energy and drives? Describe how you recognize this feature.

Take time to recall an experience of consolation. Once it is firm in your mind, what words would you use to describe your experience?

Now take time to recall an experience of desolation. Once it is firm in your mind, what words would you use to describe your experience?

If you were to begin a regular practice of the prayer of examen, when would be the best time of the day? How would you go about this? Describe your motivation or energy to do so. Is God drawing you?

What practical steps might you take to incorporate the examen into your daily life? What obstacles will you likely encounter, and how can you avoid being derailed by them?

CHAPTER 12

BEFRIENDING DESIRE

Hope deferred makes the heart sick,
but a desire fulfilled is a tree of life.

PROVERBS 13:12 (NRSV)

FOR ABOUT FIFTEEN YEARS Beth and I lived in a neighborhood built around a golf course. We didn't move there because of our love of the game, but we did appreciate the green space. In fact, each year as winter began to settle in, we looked forward to reclaiming the fairways for brisk and bone-chilling walks. The outing I recall most vividly was in January: I was alone, well-bundled and walking in the dark. The path was lit only by an icy blue moon. I was currently out of work and disillusioned with my previous three-decade career in ministry. Having just resigned from a pastoral role, a decision I did not enter into lightly, I now felt lost; two kids in college, two others in high school, with no plan B.

That night as I walked along the shadowed paths, I felt particularly alone. To make matters more disconcerting, I had been experiencing God as particularly quiet, silent even. It made no sense to me. Here I was at a crossroad and in desperate need for God to speak up and speak clearly, yet instead I heard nothing. I kept putting one heavy foot in front of the other, all the while complaining to God in frustration that his lack of speaking into my questions was confusing and disheartening. As I acclimated to the dark and the cold, my heart began to feel a bit less burdened, and I also began to detect a faint, glowing warmth inside me. When I say glow, it was more like a stirring of a subtle yet vibrant desire that ascended from my midsection, up into my head, and finally into my awareness. In my mind's eye I began to see the shape of some emerging core desires. They were consonant with older desires, but they were resurfacing as current wants and needs in this new context I found myself in.

As these thoughts began to take on more substance, I sensed God speaking quietly to my spirit. What I heard him saying was something of this nature:

> I've been waiting for you to get in touch with your own heart. Over the years your desires have merged with others' visions and priorities for your life. I've watched you drift into good things, but year by year they've taken you further from your essential self and deeper longings. I want you to stop looking outside of yourself to find clues of my will. I've been silent and moved into the shadowy background during these recent weeks so you can become reacquainted with *your* heart. I want you to realize that I've placed my will in you, and as you've gotten in touch with your deeper desires, you've gotten in touch with me and what I desire for you.

THE ENERGY OF DESIRE

In chapter 11 we considered the important question of orientation. Our orientation helps us locate our focus, our direction. In this chapter we want to consider what energizes us, specifically, how *core desires* propel and inspire us toward God and the dreams he has for us. To begin, why don't you linger with a few questions and see what it's like to consider your desires.

- When you're completely honest with yourself, what do you really want?

- In your most personal, private moments what do you deeply, ardently desire?

- If you stop trying to play the capable, responsible hero, what is it that you need?

- What longings do you have that just won't go away no matter what?

How do you feel when you read these questions? Uncomfortable? Overwhelmed? Curious? Excited? These questions can be experienced as a doorway to deeper intimacy with God, yourself, and others, *and* an unsolicited invitation to revisit past disappointments and might-have-beens. When we're alone and most in contact with our true hearts and allow these questions to surface, they can either energize us to dig beneath our day-to-day surface activity and discover a refreshing fountain within *or* leave us scurrying toward distractions and the comfortable familiarity of what is. A wellspring is an apt metaphor for this irrepressible, God-given capacity to desire. Like it or not, try as we might, ignoring our core desires is just about as effective as capping an artesian well. If you succeed in stopping the original flow, it will only burst forth in new and unwelcomed eruptions.

It seems inevitable that part of maturing and growing into adulthood is a process of coming to terms with our earnest desires. You could rightly say that children and adolescents are wanting, needing, longing beings. Just take a three year old through the checkout counter at the grocery! As we enter young adulthood, we begin to learn that some of our larger desires and needs will require that we forgo certain immediate desires and needs. In other words, we learn to moderate or deny some desires in the short run, which is evidence of growing maturity.

This is a good thing as it relates to healthy maturation and the wise pursuit of the fuller life we are being called to live. It becomes a bad thing when we begin to habitually dodge our substantial desires for lesser ones, using the lesser as fuel to get what gives immediate gratification. That's part of the problem with the consumer-oriented obsession of our culture. Desire has been co-opted as a justification for acquiring more and more and more— and getting it now!

If that weren't problem enough, most of us have also been shaped to think that our desires, as well as the very heart from which they come, cannot be trusted. Somewhere along the line, desire began to be seen through a puritanical lens and laden with sexual or erotic overtones. With these titillating associations, desire became the low-hanging fruit to which parents and authority figures leveled their not-so-veiled threats. The effect of all this is that we've inherited a strong note of inhibition around both the language of desire as well as the longings of the heart.

Finally, the case in favor of living from desire often loses its remaining credibility when we encounter the inevitable disappointment of unfulfilled desire. How often does it happen that receiving our deepest wants and needs is as simple as naming and claiming them? Isn't it more common to pine for years for their fulfillment? After you've experienced several hope-deferred moments in life, along with the heart sickness that inevitably follows, you'll realize the intelligence of the strategy "don't want, don't tell." It's safer to keep your head down and accept the scraps off the table of consumerism and the other dainties that assuage your appetites.

What we fail to see and forgo is desire's greatest value— providing a rendezvous with God. When we locate our deep, persistent, heart-oriented longings, we identify a place of God's deep presence and movement. As we vulnerably engage with God around our desires, we find solidarity and communion with Christ. *Surprisingly, we discover that desiring isn't primarily about fulfilling. Desire is a powerful spiritual energy that moves us toward God and the life we were created to live.*

PARABLES OF DESIRE

If you find yourself feeling timid about your desires, have you ever considered the theme of desire imbedded in many of Jesus' parables? Numerous times Jesus elevated persistent desire and the pursuit of its fulfillment. Read the following sampling of parables and listen for this theme.

> The kingdom of heaven is like a jeweler on the lookout for the finest pearls. When he found a pearl more beautiful and valuable than any jewel he had ever seen, the jeweler sold all he had and bought that pearl, *his pearl of great price.* (Matthew 13:45-46 *The Voice*)
>
> Imagine a woman who has 10 silver coins. She loses one. Doesn't she light a lamp, sweep the whole house, and search diligently until that coin is found? (Luke 15:8 *The Voice*)
>
> Imagine that one of your friends comes over at midnight. He bangs on the door and shouts, "Friend, will you lend me three loaves of bread?" ... Even if you didn't care that this fellow was your friend, if he keeps knocking long enough, you'll get up and give him whatever he needs simply because of his brash persistence! (Luke 11:5-8 *The Voice*)
>
> There was a judge living in a certain city. He showed no respect for God or humanity. In that same city there was a widow. Again and again she kept coming to him seeking justice: "Clear my name from my adversary's false accusations!" He paid no attention to her request for a while, but

then he said to himself, "I don't care about what God thinks of me, much less what any mere human thinks. But this widow is driving me crazy. She's never going to quit coming to see me unless I hear her case and provide her legal protection." (Luke 18:2-6 *The Voice*)

Wouldn't every single one of you, if you have 100 sheep and lose one, leave the 99 in their grazing lands and go out searching for the lost sheep until you find it? When you find the lost sheep, wouldn't you hoist it up on your shoulders, feeling wonderful? And when you go home, wouldn't you call together your friends and neighbors? Wouldn't you say, "Come over and celebrate with me, because I've found my lost sheep"? (Luke 15:3-6 *The Voice*)

In these parables, Jesus elevates desire and applauds the persistence of those who pursue the fulfillment of their desires.

- A jeweler sold all he had for a beautiful pearl.

- A woman swept her whole house and searched diligently until she found a lost coin.

- A brash man's persistence is rewarded when his neighbor gets out of bed at midnight and gives him three loaves of bread.

- An unjust judge defends a widow because she won't quit coming and seeking justice.

- A shepherd leaves his ninety-nine sheep to search for one sheep that has become lost.

What was Jesus trying to illustrate here? Isn't he emphasizing that desire is a powerful force within us that can propel us toward God and the desires God has for us? When Jesus said, "Keep on asking, and you will receive. Keep on seeking, and you will find. Keep on knocking, and the door will be opened for you" (Luke 11:9-10 *The Voice*), he was cheering you on in your desiring. He was imploring

you to desire and to turn your desires into fervent prayers that God
the Father eagerly listens and responds to. When we consider Jesus's
life and teachings we bear witness to his celebration of desire and
his admonition for us to engage our desires and seek their fulfilment
fervently and faithfully.

LOCATING THE CRUX OF DESIRE

Bernard of Clairvaux could rightly be called one of our great spiritual
theologians of desire. For Bernard, spiritual desire arises from the
heart of being human, of being alive. The heart within the breast of
each one of us can best be understood as our "organ of desire." This
doesn't mean that everything the heart desires is unqualified in its
goodness or rightness. Unquestionably, the supreme focus of desire's
desire is for God and what God loves.

So how do you grow in locating the crux of desire? How do you
recognize and consent to be moved by desire? How do you open
yourself to the gifts and the risk of meeting God in this holy and
human space within? We want to highlight four ways God graces
our personal longings, meets us in them, and influences us
through them.

*In your desires you can discern God's specific invitations and
guidance.* As you learn to befriend your desires, rather than seeing
them primarily as unruly and self-centered, you gradually begin to
welcome them for what they are: a rich, primary source of wisdom
and direction. Much like a homing device, your desires continuously send out signals and impulses that lend authenticity to the
course of your life. That's what David experienced during his late-
night walk on the golf course. He began to hear the pinging sound
of his own heart. He welcomed what he was hearing. He recognized that what was calling to him came from the deep wellspring
of desires. Gradually these desires became a source of God's direction and influence.

Paradoxically, your desires keep you grounded in the incompleteness of life. They keep speaking, not in a demanding or shaming tone but in a wise and life-affirming voice, reminding you of who you are and who you are becoming along with the features of the life you are being called to live. They keep you open to change, possibility, and the future. Were you not to heed the rich tapestry of desires, you would quickly calcify, missing the sacred invitation to grow into your full likeness of the image of God within you.

In your desires you recover your unique and essential self. Desiring can be one of our most honest, raw experiences of life. That may be one reason why we avoid acknowledging what we desire. Our desires are revealing, and sharing them may expose something vulnerable or even flawed in us. What we love, what we long for are mirrors of who we are at the deepest core of our being. As you receive knowledge of yourself through your desires, you develop a keener sense of your true authentic self. Only by paying attention to your desires and longings are you able to see into the deepest well of your heart, where you are imprinted with the image of a desiring God.

One reason your longings are such a potent source of information for your spiritual life is that there is a radical particularity about each one of your core desires. Unlike our commonly held ideals that we as Christ-followers seek to live out through Christlike principles and virtues, our individual desires vary greatly and are intrinsic to what makes me, me and you, you. Ideals and virtues exist as aspirations outside us, detached from our particular personalities and bent. Core desires, in contrast, are an expression of what *is* in you rather than what *ought* to be true of you.

In David's story something powerfully clarifying appeared as he descended into the deeper regions of his one true heart. That openness to what he truly wanted helped him differentiate from others' aspirations for him, even those he'd imagined were of God but may not have been. Risking naming these emerging desires put him back in touch with the ground of his authentic life. He now looks back on this time as a seminal moment when he recovered a renewed sense of self and the growing freedom to live from that center.

In your desires you understand the significant features of your true vocation. Not only does paying attention to your desires help you know who you really are, but they also mirror back to you how you are to live and what you are to live for. In other words, your true desires have a vocational orientation. By *vocational*, we don't mean just how you make a living or what career occupies the best hours of your day, although it does affect how you approach all this. Instead, we are suggesting that your deeper core desires inform the shape and substance of your life pursuits; your relationships, your work, your art, your interests, your service—who you are *in* this world and *for* this world at this time.

When I (David) was about to turn sixty, I had a day to myself in Saint Louis while Beth was speaking at a conference. I'd developed a recent interest in visiting historic cemeteries to photograph the statuary. Saint Louis is filled with several of these thin places. I decided to treat my day as a personal retreat in which I'd carry the simple question, What do I want my sixties to look like? And so off I went to my first site with the question floating in the background. As I was walking around, I found an ancient grotto. After climbing the stairs, I reached the top and looked out over a small field of simple tombstones marking the graves of several dozen monks. I heard, first in my mind and then I spoke it out loud, "I don't want to work for Harrison College anymore!" Taken aback by the suddenness of the thought, it was as if a clear and compelling bell had rung. I instantly knew what I wanted, or rather what I *didn't* want.

Clearly discerning your authentic vocation begins by knowing what you *don't* want as well as what you *do*. I could see clearly that my present work with the college was becoming an increasing distraction to the substance and pursuits of the life I was drawn to. As I began to make more and more space available for what I was drawn to, it became increasingly clear that my heart's desires were leading me to a vocation that was right-sized and correctly focused for me at this season of life.

In your desires, you gather into yourself God's particular fondness for you. Thomas Traherne, a seventeenth-century Anglican mystic, believed that our "wants are the bands and cement between God and us." Even a casual survey of the Old and New Testaments portrays a passionate God, a God who wants, a God with deep longings. Whatever else we do or don't share in common with God, the communion of passionate desire is a powerful and personal meeting place.

David's earlier story illustrates that our most authentic experiences of God are ones when his love is radically particularized toward us. Once God began speaking to him after the initial "gift" of God's silence, what David heard was God's familiarity with him. God was treating him as a good and wise friend. God wasn't dealing with him in a generic way, rather God was patiently and lovingly relating to him in his particular life circumstance and according to David's distinctive personality.

This kind of particular love is more akin to *eros*, one of the Greek words for love. Somewhere along the story line of Christian history, *agape love* became elevated above the more suspect and human love known as eros. Understandably, agape love conveys God's gratuitous care and commitment to humanity in spite of its slowness of heart and willful tendency to go its own ways. Agape conveys a universal, nonspecific, altruistic kind of love. It's beautiful, but at times it can feel like a mother's love. "She has to love me—she's my mother!" Yet quite remarkably even early church father Origen consistently preferred the use of *eros* in his commentaries over the more conventional word *agape* to underscore this highly personal nature of the love that God has for us. Or should we say the love God has for you?

Severing the natural bond between agape and eros love has done us a great disservice. In God, all loves are dimensions of one Love. There is no dividing line in the heart and mind of God's love for you. Unlike agape love's universality, eros love is particularized love that zooms in on you, singularly beloved as a person, uniquely wanted, desired, pursued, and prized. Opening to God's eros love keeps you honest and grounded in your core desires to be wanted, seen, felt, and loved as an individual by your Beloved.

RESPONDING TO DESIRE

In the contemplative Christian tradition, we understand that "God's yearning for us precedes and arouses our yearning for God." What an amazing thought to consider! When desire for God, attraction to God, rises up within you, it does so because it is an echo of God's desire for and attraction to you! This premise should empower and inform how we reflect on and respond to our desires.

To reflect on our desires takes time and may not happen naturally. Perhaps the best thing to do is simply force the subject. First, sit down with some good questions that help you ponder what you need and want and then see what happens. Remember the questions at the beginning of the chapter? Why not start with those?

- When you're completely honest with yourself, what do you really want?

- In your most personal, private moments what do you deeply, ardently desire?

- If you stop trying to play the capable, responsible hero, what is it that you need?

- What longings do you have that just won't go away no matter what?

Second, once you have engaged these basic questions of desire and written down responses to them, read what you've written with a contemplative attitude. Notice themes, notice strong feeling words, notice peculiar words that stand out. Then once you have noticed and named what stands out, bring those desires into prayer. Talk with God about them. Ask the Spirit to help you understand what they mean, what the invitation might be in them.

Third, be willing to sit with the desires that seem most pressing and important to consider at this time and see how Jesus speaks to you about them over time and in unexpected moments.

Fourth, listen for steps you need to take or changes you need to make as you engage with God around your desires.

There is no question that getting in touch with your desires and bringing them into prayer invigorates your relationship with God. In closing, read the following account of how a woman in a spiritual desert rediscovered her own heart and the deeper desires within.

PRAYING OUR DESIRES

While on retreat at Fall Creek Abbey, a young woman asked to meet for spiritual direction, something we make available for those we host. Jan is married and has been an elementary school teacher for a few years. In an email she said her retreat and desire to meet for spiritual direction was because she'd been experiencing spiritual dryness for some time. I (Beth) was happy to spend time listening to what was going on within her heart and life with God.

After we settled into silence for a few minutes, I broke the silence and asked what was most important for her to talk about with me. Jan began to describe her experience of feeling distant from God and in a spiritual desert for the last several months. God, at present, appeared far away and disconnected from her. I inquired about her spiritual practices, and she shared that she tried to pray and read her Bible for fifteen or twenty minutes in the morning before she left for school. "It's often rushed, and I don't really feel like it's productive, but I usually do it anyway."

I decided to ask her specifically about her prayer. "Jan, what is it like to pray? How do you experience God in prayer, and what do you find yourself praying about?"

She responded quickly and said that she prayed regularly and usually prayed about her students and the other teachers she worked with. "I want to be a good influence for Christ, and I know that most of the other teachers are not Christians." She wasn't clear about how she experienced God or if she even did. As she spoke, I wondered what really mattered to her. So, I leaned in a bit.

"Jan, if you could talk to God about anything or ask God for anything, what would it be?"

She paused for a long time and looked down. "I don't know. I'm not sure what I really want."

I responded, "So, it's hard to name your real, true desires?"

"Well," Jan responded, "I guess what I'd really ask him about—or ask him for—is a baby. That's what I *really* want! I like teaching, but I've been thinking a lot recently about how I've always wanted more than anything to be a mom."

I smiled and said, "Well, that seems like a very strong and good desire! Is that something you've brought into prayer with God—the desire to have a baby?"

Jan looked off in the distance and said with a puzzled face, "No. Not recently, anyway. And I'm not sure why."

I made the comment that when my own spiritual life and prayers feel dry, sometimes it's because I'm not engaging with God about what really matters to me. "Do you think that this could have anything to do with your experience of dryness?"

Jan wondered out loud, "Yea, I think it's very possible. I don't know why I would avoid asking God for what I really want. Maybe I'm afraid that he won't give me what I want."

"Is that what you're afraid of—that he won't answer your prayer and give you a baby?"

Jan shrugged, "I guess so. I've known so many friends who've struggled with infertility, and it's so vulnerable to feel my desire and to say it out loud and know that there's nothing I can really do about it—well, of course, except the obvious!" she blushed.

"I wonder, Jan, if it's important, whether this prayer gets answered the way you want it to or not, to bring your deep longing into prayer with God. What do you suppose would happen in your relationship with God if you did?"

Jan took some time and then slowly mused aloud, "I think my relationship with God would become more real and alive if I let him into my heart and desires. He already knows them anyway, right?"

"Yes, God does know the true and genuine desires of our hearts. And, in fact, often God is the one who awakens our desires. In spiritual direction, we consider our core desires to be a reflection of what God desires for us. What if this desire is a God stirring— an invitation for you to bring your true, vulnerable self into relationship with him through prayer and trust him? What do you think?"

Jan relaxed back in her chair, took a deep breath, and simply said, "Yes. I think so."

If you were to describe your relationship with or reaction to your desires, how would you describe it?

How do you know the difference between your deep, true desires and surface desires?

What is it like for you to think deeply about your desires? To engage in questions that elicit reflection on your desires?

What desire are you most aware of right now? How might God be in this desire you have?

When recently have you been most aware of your desire for God? Bring that moment squarely to mind and reflect on what it means that your desire was an echo of God's desire for you. What does that tell you about God's longings and desires for you?

CHAPTER 13

ENDLESSLY
INVENTIVE RESISTANCE

Only in returning to me
and resting in me will you be saved.
In quietness and confidence is your strength.
But you would have none of it.

ISAIAH 30:15

BEV AND I (BETH) SAT DOWN for thirty minutes or so after our Fall Creek Abbey peer supervision meeting for spiritual directors to talk more about a difficult professional relationship I was navigating. Bev is a friend and fellow spiritual director, so she offers a wonderful listening ear when I'm in need. As I explained some of what had happened to cause the breakdown and the accompanying feelings I was having, Bev listened intently and then said to me, "The word that keeps coming to mind is *dissatisfied*. It sounds like you're dissatisfied with the relationship." *Oh,* I thought to myself, *dissatisfied?* And then I quickly corrected her assessment and said, "More like *disappointed*."

Bev pressed in, "Really? And how do you understand the difference between the two?"

I sat for a little while and let the meaning of both words and how I experience them register within me. Soon I became aware of how quickly I dismissed the word *dissatisfied* when Bev suggested it. It was as though she'd passed me a hot potato and I quickly passed it back! And then it began to dawn on me; if I say I'm dissatisfied with something, it's on me to do something about it—to make appropriate changes, whether within myself or in the relationship. I preferred to be disappointed because it kept the responsibility for change at arm's length. Disappointment didn't cost me much, but admitting I was dissatisfied would. What I got in touch with at this moment, what my friend Bev helped me confront in myself, is something in spiritual direction that we call *resistance*. And by recognizing my resistance I was able to identify a potent place of God's beckoning presence and active Christ formation in me.

ENDLESSLY INVENTIVE EVASIONS

In her book *Spiritual Direction: Beyond the Beginnings*, Janet Ruffing titled her chapter on resistance "Endlessly Inventive Evasions." It's a great title for a subject that each of us is more familiar with than we care to admit. Every one of us has an infinite number of ways to creatively avoid that which we find uncomfortable, intimidating, or upsetting. In this chapter we want to invite you to consider looking within for those places of evasion in your relationship with life, with others, and ultimately with God. Resistance reveals the avoidance tactics we use that ultimately impede our spiritual growth and impair our ability to be open, transparent, and vulnerable human beings.

While you might be tempted right now to skip to the next chapter or put this book down altogether, we'd encourage you to take a deep breath and wait a second! Even though resistance sounds bad and is hard to talk about, it's actually a crucial phenomenon of which to become aware. That's because it marks a place where God is pressing into our lives and desiring greater intimacy with us! Resistance in our life and relationship with God "is not something to be condemned or pitied but rather welcomed as an indication that the relationship with God is broadening and deepening."

So what exactly is resistance? Resistance is an unconscious or semi-conscious rejection of something or someone that intimidates us or makes us feel anxious. What we don't immediately recognize is that this "something" is an invitation from God to be stretched and to grow; to become more transparent, self-aware, and whole. Our reaction to feeling resistant can involve any number of different tactics, including repression, denial, projection, making excuses, forgetting, getting distracted, becoming angry, or rebelling. It can, on the one hand, be mild or moderate avoidance, and on the other a formidable opposition that potentially blocks the flow of love in our relationship with God. We all employ different strategies of avoiding what threatens us, yet we do so, at least initially, without intention or awareness. Resistance is a thing.

Though resistance is a thing, it's still important to note that not all avoidance is a sign that you are resisting God's work in your life. There will be situations where resistance is called for, as in the case of someone violating a personal boundary or when you don't fully trust someone. Boundaries, preferences, precautions, and rights are not in jeopardy when addressing places of resistance.

There are, however, a number of experiences common to us that can incite our unconscious or semi-conscious resistance. A partial list follows. As you read it, notice if any bring to mind distressing experiences you recall that may have caused you to resist and react.

- resistance to growing up and maturing
- resistance to unconditional love, intimacy, or vulnerability
- resistance to greater freedom and wholeness
- resistance to change, the unknown, or what is different

- resistance to facing the realities of life

- resistance to suffering and pain

- resistance to humility or compromise

- resistance to experiencing God differently, more intimately, God as mystery

While you might read this list and think to yourself, *Why in the world would anybody be resistant to things like unconditional love, change, or humility?* The truth is, we are resistant because each of these experiences represents some form of letting down our guard. Ultimately, when we become resistant it's because we're afraid to let go of something we use to protect ourselves. For Beth, she didn't want to let go of being a victim of disappointment because being dissatisfied would require her to make changes that were painful and costly yet ultimately empowering (which, in truth, they have become).

SIGNS OF RESISTANCE

If your resistance is unconscious or semi-conscious, how can you possibly recognize it? It *is* difficult to notice on our own. Perhaps that's why resistance is discussed most often in the fields of psychotherapy and spiritual direction. It often requires the help of another to become objective about the things we involuntarily avoid. The unique and particular focus of spiritual direction is helping directees pay attention to their reactions to life, relationships, and the movement of the Spirit. More often than not these point to the fertile places of God's initiative and involvement. Once aware of those reactions, directees are then able to thoughtfully and wholeheartedly respond to God's loving work. Though a spiritual companion is helpful, there are ways that each of us can grow in noticing our own resistance toward God and God's shaping of our heart and lives.

To start, you may want to begin noticing *your body and its reactions* with more curiosity and intention. Your physical body is a brilliant source of information and is a sensitive instrument for detecting pockets of resistance, much like a barometer registering the pressure of weather patterns. Learning to recognize and distinguish when you're tense or where you feel restricted in your body is often a good early indicator. Most of us have standard physical reactions when we feel self-protective. You might feel tightness in your chest or between your shoulder blades or in your neck or throat or at your temples. When becoming aware of God pressing into a dimension of your life through a means that feels scary and uncomfortable, your muscles will likely contract in your body as a signal from the brain that you need to be on guard. Take a moment right now and scan your body; move from the top of your head through your entire midsection and limbs to the soles of your feet. Where are you aware you might be holding stress right now? Where do you typically tighten up when you feel anxious?

In addition, you will notice that in many instances your resistance can also be identified by a *quick or abrupt response* to something, even something barely registering to your conscious mind. You might quickly dismiss a thought or suggestion that comes to you from God indirectly (as in a time of prayer or reading Scripture) or directly through a friend, as was Beth's case with Bev. This backtracking, avoidance, or rationalization might even be accompanied by a subtle (or not so subtle) bout of defensiveness. "Not dissatisfied—disappointed!" In other words, your reactions feel visceral or unstoppable. The sudden, unbidden force of your reaction may point to an interior resistance toward an invitation to change or the upsetting feeling that comes from being invited to let down your guard.

Noticing your *favorite defensive moves* may be uncomfortable when you learn to read them as they telegraph the resistance you are hoping to conceal. If you encounter a situation that feels overwhelming or too much for you, you may respond by abruptly tuning out or closing yourself off—by retreating spiritually or emotionally from yourself, another, and God as well. Typically you'll observe (often in retrospect) that your overreaction doesn't match the intensity of what's actually happening. Yet instead of engaging with the situation sensibly, your walls go up as if you were being threatened by a dangerous predator.

Finally, noticing your subtle or abrupt *changing of the subject* can serve as a useful indicator of your unconscious pools of resistance. When experiencing something you instinctively know has the potential to transform you, enlarge your life, or set you free, your initial state of awareness may make you feel a bit queasy. One strategy your resistance may implement is simply to dismiss whatever you sense God bringing up. You might change the channel in your conversation with someone or even with God and talk about another problem that's more comfortable to ponder. Or you might look for your favorite object of distraction to lure your attention away rather than toward this situation or topic that God might be prompting you to consider.

Like Ruffing suggests, there is an endless number of inventive ways we evade God's invitations and sidestep uncomfortable things—yet there's also hope! By paying attention to your body and reactions you can start to recognize pockets of resistance. And once you engage the resistance by reflecting on what's really going on, then you can more clearly hear and more thoughtfully consider God's loving invitations.

Interestingly, the familiar Gospel story about a young, well-to-do ruler (Mark 10:17-22) is a wide window into the soul of someone who's resisting God and doesn't know it—that is, until he encounters Jesus. Read the following imaginative account of this fellow as if he were telling the story to his wife or a friend or even you! Notice his reactions to Jesus and see what resistance looks like in him.

Putting a Finger on Resistance

Do you remember when I went up to Jericho on business last week? As I was walking along feeling quite good about myself, I came to a roadside clogged by a horde of beggars lined up with their cups stretched out toward me. They were pitiful, really, with their dirty bodies and stench. I put a few coins in the sorriest of the group's cup and got back on the main road.

As I got my bearings, up ahead I noticed a large crowd with a cluster of children running around. I asked someone next to me what was happening, and he said that the rabbi named Jesus was visiting. I'd heard rumors of this young rabbi and was aware that a growing number of people were seriously wondering if he could be the long-awaited Messiah. So I edged up to the crowd to see him for myself. There he was holding two young children on his lap. He was telling the adults nearby that these little ones were the real heirs of God's kingdom.

I listened to what he had to say and then waited until he began walking down the street. I decided to approach him; I don't even know why. I guess I wanted to have an interaction with him and felt intrigued by what he said. So, I asked him how I could become an heir of the Lord's kingdom like the little ones he held on his lap.

It wasn't just what he said in response. It was how he looked at me. I wanted to impress him, you see, and so I told him that I'd always been faithful to the laws of God since childhood. He nodded, kept looking at me, speaking to me while staring me down—only with soft, kind, knowing eyes. I felt flustered, my body tense, and everything in me wanted to run away.

As I looked into his face, I felt exposed. He could see through my bravado, and yet strangely I didn't feel judged. I felt known, welcomed and wanted. It was disorienting. It was as if he saw things in me that I wasn't aware of. The last thing he said to me was the most troubling. He told me if I was really serious about living in the ways of God that I should sell all that I have and give the proceeds to the poor. Then I would be ready to follow him as one of his disciples.

That hit me hard! I was shocked and felt real grief. I think he was putting his finger on something much deeper though, something I haven't been able to see about myself. And that's what I can't quite shake off. All I could do at the time was walk away from him—speechless.

I haven't stopped thinking about it. As I've wrestled inside, I've become more aware of how proud and image conscious I am. I resist anything that might tarnish the "golden boy" image I have of myself. This obsession attaches itself to everything I do, everything I say to others, or even how I think about myself. The reason I'm so lost in my own world right now is that I'm seeing that world as if for the first time. I just don't know what to do about it. This life—not the one out here, the world of my image, my wealth and comfort—but this life, in here, in my heart, seems so defended. Am I making any sense?

RESPONDING (COMPASSIONATELY) TO RESISTANCE

This well-to-do young man is making a lot of sense, don't you think? For within each of us is a fortress wall of self-protection, and whenever something or someone comes close to that wall or threatens to scale the wall and find out what's on the other side, we react and resist. We've spent too much of our life protecting the goods within the fortress for fear they will be stolen or—worse yet—it's discovered that there's nothing there to steal.

Rather than provide a snapshot from a spiritual direction session on the theme of resistance, we'd like to engage this story of the rich, young ruler as if we were his spiritual director inviting him to reflect on and respond to his experience of Jesus. So, let's imagine him sitting across from one of us. He's just told us the story of meeting Jesus and ultimately walking away sad and speechless.

Our first line of questions would invite him to recall how he experienced himself during this encounter with Jesus. We might ask him, *When you were talking with Jesus, what were you feeling in your body?* We suspect he would describe feeling tense, flustered, edgy like he wanted to bolt.

Along with this, we would help him explore his full gamut of emotions: *What were your most memorable or predominant feelings?* He might share about his conflicting emotions of feeling exposed and yet not judged, feeling uncomfortable being stared through by soft, loving eyes, feeling an attraction to Jesus and anxiety that made him want to run away.

We'd want him to also reflect on his experience of how Jesus seemed to him. So, we might ask, *What was Jesus like? How would you describe your experience of him or the expression on his face?* Again, he might recall his eyes: soft, loving, yet penetrating. He might note how he felt seen and welcomed by Jesus. Hopefully, he would be able to articulate feeling loved by Jesus even though Jesus saw through his self-righteousness and pride.

We would certainly want to help him reflect on what this encounter with Jesus means to him now. *When you were with Jesus, what seemed most profound about your interaction?*

How do *you* imagine him responding to this question? He might describe the aftermath of coming to terms with his "golden boy" image and what that realization has meant to him. He might acknowledge the hard place in his heart where he feels resistant to change, to let go of this image and all the wealth that helps keep it up.

We would make room to explore with him his reaction to Jesus when he walked away sad and dejected. *What was going on inside you after Jesus asked you to sell everything and give the money to the poor?* We could imagine him describing feeling shocked and then dismayed at the cost he was asked to pay to follow Jesus. He might even be able to admit that he felt angry.

We might ask, *If you could have a do-over, how would you want to respond; what would you want to ask or say to Jesus?* At this point, he might not be able to articulate, let alone trust, that Jesus' love for him is what motivated him to recommend such a radical action. He might be able to admit that he wants to be free and live from his heart instead of out of his false self and ego, yet he is still wrestling with letting go.

When identifying resistance, it's absolutely critical to be sensitive, gracious, understanding, and compassionate to yourself. We wouldn't push this young man to get over his resistance, but instead we would encourage him to keep returning to his experience of Jesus' love. We might ask one final question, *What do you need from God right now? How will you pray?*

As spiritual director Sue Pickering writes "We can't resist a vacuum—in order to resist there must be something drawing us toward itself which we can refuse to accept—and in our directees that something is God's call to deeper relationship. Resistance, then, is an expected part of the spiritual journey; we can look at it positively as evidence that God is at work."

Resistance is a thing. And yet, as common as it is and as awkward and difficult as it is to admit and engage our resistance, it shows us the growing edge of our spiritual life and where to locate the strong, loving tug of God on our hearts.

Review the list of common experiences of resistance. Which ones do you have the most reaction to or resonance with?

What memories or current situations come to mind where you've noticed resistance within yourself?

Where do you feel resistance in your body? What does it feel like?

How do you tend to defend yourself when you are feeling resistant to something? If possible, name an example or two.

Can you identify a potential place of resistance toward God's movement in your life right now? If so, how are you presently reacting to God's initiative? How would you like to respond?

CHAPTER 14

ESSENCE AND ILLUSION

At that moment their eyes were opened, and they
suddenly felt shame at their nakedness. So they
sewed fig leaves together to cover themselves.

GENESIS 3:7

A GROWING AWARENESS OF a divided heart led me (Beth) to
seek my first spiritual director. I'd drawn a picture in my journal
one day of how I experienced the state of my own inner life and
soul. It was a heart with a jagged line down the middle separating
the two halves. On one side I wrote words that described a way of
being that I experienced some of the time—words like *whole, solid,
real, resilient, loving, genuine,* and *self-possessed.* On the other side, I
described another way I at times experienced myself: *insecure, defensive, proud, ambitious, controlling, fearful,* and *willful.* I felt extremely perplexed—even felt pain from these conflicting forces.
How could I contain both within my one self?

At the time, I didn't have the language to frame this very human
drama and dilemma—the incongruity between my true and false
selves, between my real essence and an illusory self. My heart ached
for oneness, for wholeness and integrity, instead of feeling the rub

between these two conflicting forces. Thankfully, I did know what it was like to live from the ground of my being. But I also knew all too well the sensation of extending a public persona to please and impress people as well as hide the stuff inside me I felt shame about. Sometimes I wore a mask, and at other times I lived out of the source of my belovedness. I was an enigma to myself.

This pivotal moment in my spiritual journey, when I became keenly aware of the contradiction between being and pretending, happened more than twenty years ago. As much as I would like to say that I've come home to my true self and rarely if ever struggle with my false self, that would be a lie. I still struggle (and my current spiritual director assures me that I will for the rest of life) with my false self masquerading as the "good little girl" I've worked so hard to be my whole life. And I also know the growing pleasure of being the person God created me to be and living out the implications of my true self in Christ in a genuine, loving way in the world. Let me illustrate what this struggle is like for me at this season of my life.

Not long ago I had a phone appointment prior to my appointment with Nancy, my spiritual director. While on the phone speaking with someone, I sensed the need to express a difference of opinion over a decision being made that would negatively impact me and others. My motives and the energy I was experiencing didn't feel forced or egoic, but honest and thoughtful. So, I expressed my point of view calmly *and* unapologetically. I wasn't sure how my opinion was received by the person I was talking with, but at the time I felt confident in what I expressed and how I expressed it.

I finished the phone call and left for my appointment with Nancy. While on the way, I reflected on the phone conversation and began to notice a barrage of insecure feelings, questions, and concerns about speaking up and expressing my disagreement. I was puzzled by what was happening, so during our session I shared the experience with Nancy. She listened and then calmly said to me, "Do you know who that was talking with you on your way here? Your false self. And all you need to say is, 'Thank you for trying to protect me as you've done my whole life. But I don't need you to do that anymore.'"

I have recalled and repeated her words to me that day more than I can count! My false self had been my best friend since childhood, helping to protect me and enabling me to achieve an identity by being warm, kind, competent, and compliant—a good little girl. And now that I am a big girl, a grown woman, I don't need her to play this role in my life anymore. I can find my true voice and speak that voice from the intrinsic wholeness and confidence of my true self. I can live and love and speak out of who I am in my God-created essence. As I do so, I may experience a negative reaction from others, but if I'm living from this place of integrity and strength, I won't be devastated or react defensively, as I would if my false self was being the boss.

The grand culmination of your expedition searching for signs of God in your life is this: *in finding God you find your true self*. Or as Thomas Merton puts it, "There is only one problem on which all my existence, my peace and my happiness depend: to discover myself in discovering God. If I find Him I will find myself and if I find my true self I will find Him." If your search for the presence and action of God within and all around you does not yield a discovery of your own true self in Christ, then the expedition has failed.

BEING HOSPITABLE TO BOTH SELVES

The *false self*, as David Benner describes it, is "the person we would like to be—a person of our own creation, the person we would create if we were God." You may be wondering why in the world we would do that—create a person other than the one we truly are.

Simply put, you were born into this world as an uncultivated but real self, possessing a unique essence. In addition, you were also born into a family of origin, a context. No matter how wonderful and loving your family, you still experienced the failure of human love in that context—either by not getting what you needed or by getting what you didn't need. So you developed a strategy for survival, an emergency plan.

You reached down into your essence, took hold of certain aptitudes or traits that resided there and exaggerated them (while diminishing others), and began to build a self you thought had a better chance of getting what you needed or could protect you from getting what you didn't need. (This is all done quite unconsciously.) Recall Beth's story of how she had created her "good little girl" false self in order to navigate life. Beth found her God-given abilities to be personable, hard-working, caring, and other-centered and exaggerated them, becoming obsessed with overcaring and overachieving. This led to a life of compulsive people pleasing and performing for love and approval.

The true self, on the other hand, is the person God created you to be. It's the person God has known for all eternity, the person God willed into existence and who has always been—and forever will be—loved by God. The true self is where the seed of Christlikeness is planted (1 John 3:9) and is the only self that bears the image of God (Genesis 1:27). This is the one self that can know and relate to God. However, the true self isn't perfect—not in the way we usually think of perfect—but it is whole and intact and resilient. It is the person you truly are as well as the person you are becoming. We haven't fully embraced all that it means to be our true selves, yet the potential is within us to do so.

The secret to knowing the false and true self is to be hospitable to both as you observe their forces at work in your inner life. If you react with resentment, judgment, or anxiety when you notice your unhealthy patterns at work, you will shame the false self into hiding. Instead, acknowledging how it served you during your growing-up years and thanking it, as Nancy encouraged Beth to do, is a much more helpful approach. However, you do need to "decisively dismiss it" from being your boss any longer so that space is created for the full flowering of your real essence. If you want to be on the lookout for God, you will simultaneously be on the lookout for your original self. Summarizing the words of many ancients, David Benner writes, "There is no deep knowing of God without a deep knowing of self, and there is no deep knowing of self without a deep knowing of God."

THE NATURE OF ESSENCE AND ILLUSION

Becoming a student of your own interior life is critical to becoming the person God created you to be. It's essential to become aware of what it feels like to live from your true essence and what it feels like when you're wearing a mask. Only then can you open up to God's transforming work in your life, a work that enables you to put off the illusory garments you've clothed yourself in and "put on the new self, created to be like God in true righteousness and holiness" (Ephesians 4:24 NIV).

In order to become familiar with the nature of the false and true self, let's return to the beginning of our human story, which is described in the Judeo-Christian creation story in Genesis 1–3. It commenced in a garden, a paradise, where the original couple had everything going for them until they breached a God-given boundary. This crucial choice initiated a disconnection not only between them and God but also a disconnection between their original selves and their fig-leaved false selves. Imagine the original couple trying to describe the before and after of paradise and paradise lost. What was it like in their original selves to walk with God in the cool of the evening? And what it was like after they rejected God's guidance and experienced shame and the need to hide?

Before and After

When we first walked among the lush trees and vegetation of the garden, we were eager to explore everything because it was so new and verdant, and we were so free, curious, and un-inhibited. Ours was a world of unhindered being and doing. With all of our senses we drank in the sweet nectar of life and worked tirelessly each day in the rich soil of Eden. Cultivating all the varieties of fruits and vegetables became a satisfying task, and the bounty on our table was an incredible delight!

Much of life we were side by side, deepening the bond between us. We laughed and played; talked endlessly, and could enjoy each other's company in absolute silence. Then when nightfall came we held each other closely, exploring the mystery and ecstasy of sexual union, a gift that forged oneness between us and deepened our love.

Elohim was always close by, and we often walked together at night as the sun set and the temperatures cooled. We talked freely together. There was nothing we couldn't ask and nothing he wouldn't tell us. It was an easy relationship, and we enjoyed the consolation of his presence. We certainly understood the clear boundaries he gave us, though admittedly our curiosities were piqued. What was so off-limits about the tree in the middle of the garden? It looked like all the others. At that time we had no fear because we felt secure with Elohim. And we honestly had no fear of ourselves. Innocence was blissful, and now we look back with such profound regret.

It happened unexpectedly. The serpent approached and planted an idea in our minds that had never occurred to us. Could something be missing from our lives, from our utopia? Yet his arguments were cunning, and something about his taunt made us feel like we wanted to prove him wrong. Plucking the fruit from the tree was easy. And though we wondered and waited, no lightning struck and no ground swallowed us up. In fact, nothing really happened at first.

The change began subtly. It started with the feeling of discomfort, even in our own bodies. We went about our day planting and pruning yet became increasingly agitated, self-conscious, feeling insecure. Something we now know to be our conscience was racked with guilt and we felt ashamed and full of regret. Eve thought of it first. She searched for some large, sturdy leaves to stitch together to cover our bodies. They didn't really help us feel better—except maybe less vulnerable than when we were stark naked.

Then we heard Elohim walking in the garden like the Lord always did, calling out to us and inviting us to join him. We panicked. What should we do? Strangely, we felt defensive toward our Creator and decided to hide, pretending we weren't home. And we really weren't home—not home within ourselves as we'd once been.

The homesickness we felt at first was almost unbearable. Yet over time, we've gotten used to our fig leaves and now we wouldn't go anywhere without them.

Represented within this fictional account of Genesis 3 is a description of what it might have been like for the original couple to have experienced life before and life after they violated God's instructions and were cast from the garden. The fig leaves, a metaphor of the false self, represent their attempt to cover their shame with a flimsy layer of self-protection. And that's exactly what we attempt to do when we assemble our own array of leaves to create the costume of our false self. Reflecting on the nature of our own essence and illusion through the lens of this story, consider four descriptive contrasts between the false and true self.

THREATENED VERSUS SECURE

If there's one tell-tale sign that reveals the nature of the false self, it's the sensation of being threatened and defensive. Because the false self is really an illusion, a ghost, lacking substance, it doesn't want its cover blown. Picture the Great Wizard of Oz before the curtain is pulled back to reveal a fumbling old man. When you live out of your persona, though you may appear large and in charge, behind the mask the false self is insecure, guarded, anxious, and self-protective. You see this in the original couple after they disobeyed God's instructions to them. They hid from Elohim because they felt self-conscious about their nakedness, insecure in their relationship with God, and ashamed of what they'd done. Eventually, they blamed each other and the serpent, all because the false self deflects when threatened with the fear of exposure.

When you live from your true self, however, you certainly are put on alert by threatening situations, yet you also experience the reality of being rooted in the abiding love and presence of God. Your roots in love keep you grounded during the storms of life. You feel your branches swaying, but you also experience the secure attachment you have to God and God has to you. Like the original couple, in your true self you enjoy a comfortable and secure relationship with God. You know that God sees you in your nakedness; nothing is hidden from God's view, including all your sins and secrets. Yet in your vulnerability you can—from your authentic being—surrender to God and trust God's love, forgiveness, and acceptance of you.

COMPULSIVE VERSUS MEASURED

Though we don't care to admit it, we all have compulsive behaviors, and in fact they are what we use to keep our false self pasted up. Overcaring, overindulging, overcontrolling, overimproving, over-achieving—each of these over*somethings* are our exaggerated efforts

to keep up the image we want to have of ourselves and want others
to have of us. We overindulge to maintain the image of being carefree,
fun-loving, and flamboyant. We overcontrol to maintain the image
of being strong, having it together, and being on top of everything.
We overimprove to maintain the image of being conscientious, exceptional, and better than other less-disciplined people. Consider
the story again of that fateful moment when the original couple eyed
the tree and began to covet the mouth-watering, wisdom-granting
fruit. Something happened in that split second when they caved to
the suggestion that their utopia was lacking a quality that this fruit
could provide. They ate it. And we all keep eating it, over and over
and over again.

When you live out of your true self, your overexaggerated, compulsive tendencies are simply not in operation. You may work hard,
very hard, yet your movements, actions, and interactions are measured. Your initiations and responses are unhurried. Living from
this center doesn't feel forced, obsessive, or out of control. Instead,
you feel healthy energy and purposeful engagement flowing from
you. Sometimes people call it "living in the flow." Others call it
"being in the zone." These phrases suggest that when you are living
from your real self you will live actively but not frantically. When
living from your true essence, you are free to choose the way of God
rather than be hijacked by the compulsions of the false self in its
attempts to keep up appearances.

WILLFUL VERSUS WILLING

While compulsivity suggests the habit of making unconscious,
passive choices, the false self is also extremely willful in its efforts to
maintain dominance. Because we have created our idealized self
from our own assessment of the person we need to be in order to
make life work, to keep ourselves safe, to acquire the accolades we
crave, the false self maintains rigorous control through its own

stubbornness. It, in truth, is *very bossy*. It is demanding and wants total and complete allegiance. Don't you see that in the original couple's response to God once their eyes were opened to their nakedness and they felt shame? God called out and asked them to join him, and they felt defensive, eventually telling God that they were hiding because they were naked and felt afraid of the Lord. (What had God ever done to make them afraid?) God asked if they'd eaten the fruit, and they quickly placed the blame on each other and the serpent. There's no admission of wrongdoing. They refused to take responsibility for their actions. The false self willfully pushes that off in order to protect itself from exposure.

The true self knows it doesn't need to prove itself or protect itself because it exists in the security of Christ's love. In your essence there is the capacity to be honest and truly repentant: the ability to care, love, serve, recede, and even lose for the good of another. Your original self bears the image of God (Genesis 1:27), is rooted in the love of God (Ephesians 3:17), and truly delights in serving God, who it knows and loves (1 John 3:9-10). If you hope to live aligned with the will of God for your life, only your true self can willingly submit to God because it knows God is good, God is loving, and God is your eternal home.

HOLLOW VERSUS SOLID

The false self conceals at all costs that it is hollow at its core. And so when we live from it, we fear—which is often repressed—that if we're not careful, this hollowness or emptiness might be found out. When we attend to our interior life, we experience a sensation of our false self as vaporous, superficial, a façade. And yet because we invest so many years in projecting this image we've created, we now totally identify with it. It's like the pastor we once heard who acknowledged with sadness that his church had hired his false self! The original couple was booted out of the garden because of their mutiny. But that wasn't their greatest loss, which was losing touch with their substantial and real selves as they lost touch with God. They became a facsimile of the persons God had created them to be as they began to live at a distance from their true selves. From that point on, the reflection of God's image and glory dimmed (Genesis 5:3).

There is a solid, substantial feel to the real you, however. You know intuitively that it is genuine and is the core of who you are and who you were created to be by God. Because your true self exists in relationship to God, like the vine connected to the branch, you know that the life of God flows through you. You are at home in your true self, and home is a very solid, settled place to be.

In the following spiritual direction session with Philip, one of David's directees, Philip is finally able to articulate why he finds it so difficult to be alone. He fears that if he becomes completely still and silent, he will discover that he is actually hollow on the inside, that there's no one home.

THERE'S NO ONE HOME

After a few minutes of silence, Philip brought up what he wanted to discuss—his continued difficulty in spending time with God in silence and solitude. He shared that whenever he is home alone, he fills the space with some kind of noise: he listens to a podcast or turns on music or the television in the background, or he mindlessly searches the internet for news feeds or articles around his latest interests. David asked Philip to contemplate for a few minutes the question, What am I afraid will happen in the silence?

"Well, what comes to mind is not so much an answer to the question but an awareness of the uncomfortable sensation I have in my body. I feel so agitated when I sit still and everything is completely silent. I feel like I'm going to jump out of my skin!"

"That sounds pretty awful," David replied. "Have you discovered *anything* that helps you relax your body and be still and open to the silence?"

"Sometimes when I take walks in nature I begin to settle down and can pray a little. That does help. It's almost like I enter silence through the backdoor and feel less anxious about being there," Philip explained.

"Philip, do you have any idea, any hunch, why you feel so reticent to be quiet and still? What is going on in your thinking? Or what are your unconscious, maybe unacknowledged, thoughts?" David asked. "And take your time to answer."

Philip sat for a few moments, his eyes diverted as though concentrating and reflecting. He slowly, almost cautiously began to speak: "As strange as it sounds, I think I'm afraid to be alone with myself because I may discover that, deep down, I'm empty. There's no one there. No one at home."

"Ahh," David nodded. "That seems important to acknowledge. So, if no one is at home inside you, then who is the person living your life?"

Philip paused and shook his head. "I don't know. It's the person I think I need to be—you know—in my work, my friendships, as a Christian."

David smiled and nodded. "What if the emptiness you feel really belongs to a self-image of your own creation? But the truth is you have a true and real self, a self who God created and knows and loves, and that self is anything but empty and hollow. What do you know about your real self?"

Philip thought for a moment and then responded, "I'm not sure. But when you mentioned that I do have a real self that God created and knows and loves, I felt something inside me respond—like something woke up. I guess it's possible that there is someone home. I just don't know who it is."

Like Philip, many of us have spent most of life forming an identity around external factors like our appearance, performance, security, competency, or mastery of life. The unfortunate truth is that we are looking for rich treasure outside ourselves when the real treasure exists within. This is such an enduring human dilemma that even St. Augustine from the fourth century echoes the lament, "I came to You late, O Beauty so ancient and new. I came to love You late. You were within me and I was outside where I rushed about wildly searching for You like some monster loose in Your beautiful world."

RESPONDING TO ESSENCE AND ILLUSION

"We do not find our true self by seeking it. Rather we find it by seeking God." Looking within, while often intimidating and discouraging will eventually yield a beautiful harvest of knowing both God and your true self, which was created to be like God. This harvest comes through the patient and lifelong process of intentional reflection and meaningful response to God's liberating work within.

Pay attention. This process begins by paying attention to the quality of your thoughts, feelings, and actions and noting if they resemble the threatened, compulsive, willful, and hollow false self or if they resound with the secure, measured, willing, solid essence of the true self. The most effective step toward liberation from the false self is to catch it in action. When you become familiar with the face of your false self, then you can address it with compassion and authority. "Thanks for seeking to protect me, but I don't need your help anymore."

Recognize sensations. It's every bit as important to recognize the sensation of living out of your true self as it is to recognize the impostor. So in the same way, the most effective step toward living from your true self is to notice it in operation in real time. Reflect on what it feels like to live from that center of your being. Notice how it feels in your body, what quality your thoughts seem to have, and how your emotions feel when they resonate from this deep, true place within you.

Write, draw, journal. All reflection is enhanced through writing, drawing, or journaling. Take time to find words that help you describe most vividly how you feel when you're fully alive, living from your authentic self. And do the same as you seek to describe the patterns of your false self. It might be helpful to ask, When did these false self patterns begin and what are they trying to accomplish? As you reflect on your true self, ask, In what environments or situations do I feel most alive and aware that I'm living authentically?

Seek help. While becoming familiar with these false-self patterns is critical to being freed from them, the value of seeking help from a professional counselor or spiritual director can't be underestimated. Meeting with a counselor is not just reserved for those whose lives are falling apart. It's actually normative for anyone seeking greater wholeness and freedom in their lives. Meeting with a spiritual director is also a spiritual practice for anyone who truly desires objective assistance in his or her formational journey.

Consent to God's work. As you become a student of your interior life and your true and false ways of being, you are poised to consent to God's transformational work within you. Not surprisingly, you will discover that the false self cannot heal itself. In other words, you won't become whole (your true self) through human effort and exertion to reform the false self. Wholeness is the outcome of consenting to God's deep, mysterious awakening in the core of your being. Once you taste the freedom of living in Christ from your true center and your increased desire and consent to die to the antics of your false identity, you will only want more freedom, more wholeness, more of Christ! "My old self has been crucified with

Christ. It is no longer I who live, but Christ lives in me. So I live in this earthly body by trusting in the Son of God, who loved me and gave himself for me" (Galatians 2:20).

Finally, as hard as it is to acknowledge, if you fail to discover your true self, then you really have no self to engage with God and respond to God's personal overtures of love for you. For the only self that God knows and draws to God's self is your true or original self, the self you were created by God to be. If in your mission to discover more of God you fail to uncover more of your authentic self, you will ceaselessly struggle to live out the implications of your relationship with God, let alone in your interpersonal relationships and the broader community. You will have no capacity for authentic love because only your true self can truly love.

Why do so many today weigh and find wanting the Christians they encounter? Could it be that even a religious false self is still merely a self-protective illusion? We have come to the conviction that the most compelling apologetic for the Christian faith is found in the lives of individuals who live from their genuine essence! This is what the world needs to see in order to take notice and become curious about Jesus: people fully human and fully alive revealing the radiance of Christ's light through their unique personhood.

What do you know about your false self? What do you notice when you are living from your false self? Describe your feelings, thoughts, and bodily sensations.

What do you know about your true self? What do you notice when you are living from your true self? Describe your feelings, thoughts, and bodily sensations.

How has knowing God helped you know yourself? And how has knowing yourself helped you know God?

What have you discovered that helps you to live more consistently from your true self in Christ?

CHAPTER 15

NIGHT WORK

And I will give you treasures hidden in the darkness—secret riches.
I will do this so you may know that I am the LORD,
the God of Israel, the one who calls you by name.

ISAIAH 45:3

IT HAPPENS WITH SUCH frequent repetition it barely registers anymore. Night follows day, just as surely as day follows night. We accept without contest the days shortening and the nights lengthening in our march toward the winter solstice. Even those living in Reykjavík, Iceland, have adjusted to twenty hours of darkness at winter's peak. But when it comes to the psychological, emotional, and spiritual experience of life lived in light's absence, each one of us is naturally disoriented and confused. Our illuminated imaginations formed in daylight seem as useless as ancient maps representing the world's edges with drawings of dragons and sea monsters. Who in their right mind would want to sail there? And yet the irresistible and unbidden tides of our lives carry us into these dark regions repeatedly throughout life's long voyage.

If we look for insight regarding this obscure phenomenon in much of spiritual formation literature today, we would instead find information that largely deals with our part in the spiritual life, the activities and spiritual practices that seemingly assure us we will arrive at the destination of Christlikeness (largely because *we* have determined it to be so). We could call this "day work." It is the active side of our formation. This is without question an important dimension of the spiritual journey, but at best day work is only half of the formational trek.

What we may not realize is that day work's contribution to our spiritual progress may be far less determinative in our spiritual growth than its complement, "night work." In night work, we are largely passive and unaware of the hidden but efficacious work of God deep in the regions of our souls. Night work in the spiritual life is not dependent on what we do and is totally dependent on the wise, gracious, and loving movement of the Spirit at the center of our being. Consider the perspective of Jeremiah, the weeping prophet in the Old Testament, who bears witness of this working in the dark.

Working in the Dark

His hands trembled slightly as he reached for the scroll hidden under his bed. Was it old age or the memory of the experience recorded on it that shook him so? Jeremiah's prophetic work had all been recorded and passed on to the community to help them remember. He was known among them as their "weeping prophet." And they likely knew only half of the tears he'd shed. But for some reason he'd held back this small scroll. It was both more personal, more heartbreaking, and at the same time more comforting to him. On the border in large letters he'd simply scrawled the word *Lamentations*.

As he pondered the words, he also recalled the events, the smells, the cries of a city falling to its enemies. It was painful to relive this period of his life, but the physical and emotional trauma seemed like nothing compared to the spiritual trauma

he endured. As his eyes skimmed over the graphic-worded attempts to rectify the justice (or was it injustice?) of what had
occurred, his reading slowed at certain places that raised
deeper, more enduring questions of the hidden, dark work
of God.

*"Lonely is this city that once bustled with life; cheer is empty;
like a widow she is abandoned, and oh, so lonely."* Abandoned,
that's what it felt like. That's what it was like. *"Her former friends
ignore her; there is no one there to share her sorrow."* Alone and
isolated, he recalls the utter absence of human comfort. People
around him were struggling to survive, and some still hung on
to their religious platitudes, compounding Jeremiah's anguish.
His heart was softer toward them now. They were terrified,
looking for any scrap of flotsam in the midst of the dark storm
they were enduring.

Continuing to read, his eyes fell on the words: *"Gone are the
days that she remembers, happy and precious; Jerusalem
wanders aimlessly and remembers what precious things she has
lost—things from the old days."* Although it was Jerusalem's experience, now Jeremiah sees it was his experience as well. He
was Jerusalem. He had lost the old ways of worshiping God as
everything was stripped from him. *"Summoning my lovers
brings nothing—nothing but pain in their betrayal. The old guard,
religious and political leaders, had died starving in the city."* Not
only had the old ways of seeking God failed; the carriers of joy
and protection were no more. It's as if those who were once a
life-giving stream simply dried up and disappeared.

But worst of all was that his sense of God had vanished.
*"Felling his own dwelling like a garden hut, God destroyed His
meeting place; He did away with the sacred festivals and Sab-
baths in Zion. . . . He disdained the most sacred religious spots,
his altar, his sanctuary, the centerpiece of our tradition."* Jeremiah recalls how proud they were of their faith. Actually not so

much their faith but how faithful they were to their traditions and laws. In retrospect he sees how they had confused their religious practices and the feelings it evoked with their real identity as people of the living God.

Pausing now, he reflects on what the experience wrought in him. It was a dark time, and he would never choose to repeat it. Yet something had shifted. He was less proud, less certain, less in control, and amazingly his faith and devotion to God had somehow survived. That small flame that had always been inside remained and the experience had purified him of other lesser loves.

As he closed the scroll and was ready to entrust it to the community, his eyes were drawn to these words that still rang clear in his old ears, *"How enduring is God's loyal love; the Eternal has inexhaustible compassion. Here they are, every morning, new! Your faithfulness, God, is as broad as the day. Have courage, for the Eternal is all that I will need. My soul boasts, 'Hope in God; just wait.'"* Twilight had turned to midnight; a long, dark midnight. And God in the dark, hidden places was doing his night work, graciously and steadily setting us free.

And now, dawn had come and with it renewed hope.

TRUSTED GUIDES OF THE DARK NIGHT

The regions we are exploring in this final chapter have perhaps been most thoughtfully explored by two doctors of the interior life, Teresa of Ávila and Saint John of the Cross. Threads of reflection on the perceived absence and withdrawal of God appear in the writings of others before them, but the sophistication, nuance, and attention they acquired through observing their own and other's spiritual experiences reached a peak in their timeless bodies of work. The phrase "dark night of the soul" can be clearly attributed to John, who wrote a poem of the same title followed by its lengthy commentary. The Spanish word John used was *oscura*. If it sounds to you like the word *obscure*, you're right. The *noche oscura* is when the face of God, the presence of God, the comfort that God bestows on us becomes obscured.

This unchosen phenomenon results in the radically unpleasant sensation of God's supportive and tangible presence receding; as if God has moved away. It's an experience of sheer absence, silence, even abandonment. How in the world could that be a good thing? How could God be in (or rather not in) this night work? What is most striking, as well as most surprising to those who have not read the poem, is that the dark night is not represented by John as a sinister, foreboding, or negative time. Rather, it has a deep and loving purpose that prepares the way for the consummate experience of union between the Beloved and his lover, of achieving increased freedom to be loved and to love, now unencumbered by the attachments and compulsions of lesser loves.

John and Teresa writing five hundred years ago did not have access to the psychological or neurological insights we possess today. And most of us have never lived in a monastic context like theirs, where life revolved around seeking God in prayer. While deeply indebted to John and Teresa, our approach in this chapter is not strictly aligned with their technical understandings of the dark night. Nor are we using the term *dark night* in the sense of its more popular and ad hoc reference as simply "going through a bad patch." What we are seeking to illuminate is the distinct spiritual experience of "being in the dark" in terms of God's presence and action in our lives.

HELLO DARKNESS MY OLD FRIEND

Without the insights and guidance wrought from others' costly and personal experience of God's work in the darkness, few of us would be aware of or openly consent to this painful, hidden process. Thankfully we have such teachers in John and Teresa, along with others, who can offer some steady guidance. Before we illuminate the gifts and purposes of this night work, we'd like to describe a few features to help you better recognize these obscure experiences. Following Gerald May's synthesis of John's themes, there are three consistent signs that often indicate that we are traversing a dark night experience.

1. Dryness and lack of energy for prayer as well as other aspects of one's spiritual life. We've already considered the experience of consolation in the spiritual journey. During night work, consolation in prayer has seemingly evaporated. There is none of the peace, hope, or joy formerly experienced in times of silence, solitude, or worship. Rather, there is an arid experience of nothing happening or, even worse, a palpable sense of God's absence, even of God's abandonment. The corresponding sensation of this experience is more akin to desolation rather than consolation.

This hue can color the rest of your life as well. Life feels like a burden, things that once mattered lack luster, and relationships that were once a source of joy seem empty and shallow. You can find this experience honestly recorded in many of the psalms. "My soul *is dry and* thirsts for You, . . . as a deer thirsts for water" (Psalm 42:1 *The Voice*). "My soul thirsts for you; my whole body longs for you in this parched and weary land where there is no water" (Psalm 63:1 NLT*)*. Your thirst remains but quenching your thirst simply doesn't happen. As John of the Cross described this juncture, there is "no consolation in things of God or created things either."

2. Lack of meaning or satisfaction in the old ways. To add to the disconcerting nature of a dark night, you may also feel bewildered by the diminished satisfaction from sources of nurture and support that previously carried you along. What does it mean that you now question some beliefs you once held certain and sacred? What's happening to you when you experience your close spiritual companions as superficial or find yourself irritated by their clichés? Why do you have less desire to serve others and offer your gifts and time to the mission that had been so central to your life purpose? How can it be that your tried and true spiritual practices have become so devoid of life? Keeping with the image of night work, you now find yourself in a time of twilight, a time of inescapable transition when everything that was once seen so clearly by daylight is now blurred, indistinct, and unidentifiable.

Even though Jesus warns us that we cannot put new wine into old wineskins, the experience of being stripped of our old wineskins reveals how stubbornly attached we are to *them* rather than to the *rich, new wine.* This unsettling aspect of a dark-night experience can make you feel like you're regressing or even losing your faith. You may redouble your efforts to get back on track, but sooner or later you realize that you really don't want the old ways. Unsure of what you do want, you know you can't continue to live out of duty and habit any longer. You may even feel like a betrayer of God, your friends, and your tradition. Gerald May describes the inner torment of the experience this way: "The person has by no means forgotten God, but rather remembers God with great pain and grief."

3. A simple, dogged desire for God somehow persists. Perhaps most surprising of all and indicative of the genuine purpose of night work is that love for God is preserved. It's like the untouchable life within a pine cone that closes up during a forest fire. In a protective gesture, the seeds draw together in order to withstand the scorching blaze. Later when the earth cools and the rains come, the regeneration of life miraculously continues.

In spite of all the perceived losses, confusions, and stripping that occur during the dark night, the kernel of the soul's dogged love for God is preserved. And even more, it is purified and set free. This may be the surest sign of the dark night; it is ultimately not about subtraction but rather about increasing your fervor for and attraction to the Lover of your soul.

GIFTS OF THE NIGHT

So what exactly is going on in us as we journey through these dark night experiences? On one hand, since it obscures the activity of God, there is likely much we won't understand. It is God's private business to do the night work in the depths of our souls. Even though we'd prefer to be in control of our lives, there's something strangely comforting and freeing to know that God is at work beyond our efforts to reform ourselves. But knowing a bit about the procedure we are undergoing can help us settle in and not resist this mysterious process. *What exactly does night work accomplish in us that our day work often leaves untouched?*

This is where more recent psychological insights about unhealthy attachments, compulsions, and addictions can translate to our modern minds what John was seeking to convey. As Gerald May puts it, "The dark night is a profoundly good thing. It is an ongoing spiritual process in which we are liberated from attachments and compulsions and empowered to live and love more freely." At its core, the hidden, obscure work of God in the dark night is both setting you free and calling you to increased freedom to love and be loved. As a result of the many dark nights you will encounter during your lifetime, you can hope someday to become consumed with love, even as God is love.

John Coe offers a wonderful illustration to help us understand what the process accomplishes. When we are new in our spiritual journey, we are like a vulnerable and needy newborn, and God graciously offers us many spiritual comforts and supports. We're like a baby who learns to trust her mother to feed her when she's hungry. God generously condescends to the needs of our spiritual longings during this phase of our lives.

However, at a certain point, every mother knows that she, along with her beloved child, will need to be weaned. The infant daughter may become confused, frustrated, even hysterical. Coe describes the parallel in our spiritual lives as God taking the "bottle of spiritual pleasures" away. Those consistent experiences of spiritual consolation have become too important. They are actually in danger of becoming an idol, replacing the person of God with God's gifts.

In today's language we are developing an unhealthy attachment to good yet finite things and turning them into absolute and ultimate things we mistakenly come to believe we must have in order to survive. And so God, in ways that often obscure our assurance of his goodness, initiates a process of withdrawal. What happens inside of our grown-up self is no less confusing than the uncontrollable desolation of a child being weaned. God is diminishing our experience of his presence and immediate support as a means of loosening our attachments, compulsions, and addictions.

There are four discernible phases of this weaning process according to Bernard of Clairvaux, a twelfth-century French abbot. However, remember night work is primarily God's work, and we often may not even be aware of its effect until we look back.

To start with, we all begin life with what Bernard described as a "love of self for self's sake." There is nothing wrong with this part of our journey. Likely without it, we wouldn't survive long past childhood. We come to learn that we are a self. We learn to take care of our self. We even cherish our self and commit to doing whatever it takes to help it thrive. And then, at some point, we realize that life is big and uncertain; and we are small and vulnerable.

God, on the other hand, is even bigger, capable, loving, and caring. God seems like a useful and important ally to have on our side. So we enter into a phase of our spiritual journey where we "love God for self's sake." We become increasingly adept at navigating what we perceive God likes and doesn't like. We really do love God, but in a childish, transactional sort of way. God condescends and cooperates in order to teach us that he is in fact loving, forgiving, and attentive. But loving God for the sake of self is not a mature relationship. In fact it can leave us compulsively in search of our next high, our next spiritual fix. And if that doesn't work, we are at risk of returning to the soothing pleasures of the created world to satisfy our cravings for unholy or unhealthy gratification.

Now the night work emerges not only as a profound episode (often how it's portrayed) but equally as an obscure and close companion, confronting the strategies we use to get God to meet our needs. Little by little these dark-night experiences begin to liberate us so that we can increasingly "love God for God's sake." We no longer simply love God for what God can do for us or for how God makes us feel. The consolation and gifts God gives are becoming less and less our primary focus. Increased freedom to love and be loved is quietly taking over our lives.

Many would stop here. What could be more desirable than loving God for God's sake? Bernard completes the circle, however, and describes the other side of loving God for God's sake; we enter a fuller expression of our humanity and begin to "love self for God's sake." Somehow, the mysterious process of severing our attachments and compulsions has left us free to look in the mirror and see who God sees. And rather than worship or despise what we see, we begin to love ourselves in concert with the love we find in God's eyes.

Consider this vignette of James, one of David's directees, who has unintentionally entered the process of night work. Notice what it is like for him to feel lost in the dark and begin to find his way through it.

LOST IN THE DARK

In our previous meeting, James talked about some recent anxiety and discontent he'd been experiencing. This was a new development for him, and it seemed quite confusing. As we settled into our time, I wondered if he would return to that theme.

James   Well, let me line up a few things for you and then we'll see if there's anything in them. I'm really excited about this opportunity that's come to me. I have these three new friends/partners, and we all have a strong sense that we've come together to launch a social-venture enterprise. It feels like an answer to prayer, even though I'm not sure I've been praying for it.

David   Isn't that like God to go ahead of us even when we're not seeking?

James   It really does feel like that. I'm not sure how I'm going to juggle it all, but this seems like something I'm to give myself to. The other issues I'd like to lay out seem more confusing. As I've mentioned before, I've been more anxious and drained by some of the activities that used to bring me life. For instance, when I'm serving at church I feel like I can't wait until it's over and I can go home. I know the need for people to serve is huge right now, but I crave some space, some quiet—some time for me. And then there's our small group. I've always loved our group and the people in it. Some of them have moved away, and while I care about the people that remain, I feel like we're the givers. My wife and I know that if we leave the group it will probably disband, but my heart is just not in it anymore.

David   You sound pretty weary and deenergized by these things, James. How do you feel about feeling this way?

James   Conflicted. On the one hand I feel incredibly lame. I've always been hyperresponsible. So for me, I feel guilty, like I just need to tough it out and quit complaining. On the other hand, I really, really don't want to. It's like the things that once brought me joy and helped me move closer to God are now like a rock in my shoe. I just want to sit down and dump it all out. Does that make sense?

David   I think it does. You probably feel like you're losing something, yet you don't have the energy or the will to try to hang on to it either. James, let's assume for a minute that there's not something wrong, either with you or your church. Let's assume that God is quite possibly up to something in all this. How does that sit with you?

James   (*taking his time to answer*) I've wondered something like that. Not exactly the same but similar. So, let me back up and give a little context. You know, my wife and I got married early. We had kids and successful careers—boom, boom, boom! We kept up with the fast ride and even became vital people in our church. Everything seemed to turn to gold, and we give God credit. But now, it seems hollow and empty. I don't know if I'm burned out, but I can't keep living this way. When you say that God might be in this in some way, what do you mean?

David   James, what if I told you that what you're experiencing is a normal part of our spiritual journey. It actually might be evidence that God is operating beneath the surface of your life in ways you can't control; that God is doing God's work independent of your efforts. What would you say to that?

James   That would feel like a relief, actually. I think I'm not only tired from my commitments at church; I'm weary of having to carry the weight of my spiritual life on my own shoulders. The thought that God might actually be doing something in me that is independent of my efforts sounds amazing. It's funny, in spite of the weariness in my soul, I still want God. Maybe even more than ever! I'm really aware of it when I'm with my three business partners and we're talking about our new venture. It doesn't just feel like the adrenaline of a new thing but a dawning of something of God that is less cluttered and encumbered by my ego.

David   James, I think God just might be setting you free. You see, freedom in our life with God isn't an end in itself. Freedom is a gift, but it's a gift that unleashes us to love God, to love others, to love ourselves. I wonder if God just might be setting you free from what has been holding you back.

RESPONDING TO NIGHT WORK

Night work is designed to loosen your grip on the countless objects, aims, and ways that your attachments keep you caged. Night work is God's way of getting to the root of things. So how can you cooperate with God's deep, hidden work in you? Following the three signs outlined previously of a dark-night experience, we would like to suggest a few broad and generous ways to reflect and respond.

Don't give up. First, as prayer becomes drier, it's important to not give up on prayer. You might reflect on your recent experience of prayer and any new or different ways you are being drawn to pray. God may be transitioning you from prayer as meditation to prayer as contemplation. Classically, meditation is a more active form of prayer that involves thinking, reflecting, asking, and wrestling.

Contemplation is a less-worded, less-striving movement in prayer. What if you were to respond to this dryness by simply being with God and resting in prayer with God rather than trying hard to pray or just scrapping prayer altogether?

Pull back. As the desire for the old ways diminishes or even disappears, this is the time to cooperate with the hidden work of God by pulling back, taking a break from your fixed spiritual practices or certain ways of thinking, relating, or serving in the ways you have in the past. The absence of these forms can be both freeing and disorienting. We must be patient with the process and let go of compulsively saying yes to what our hearts no longer desire, trusting that new ways, new forms, and new relationships will come along if we wait and remain open. Take time to reflect on what you need to take a break from and then respond by doing what you need to do to be released from these obligations.

Be with God. Finally, as you note the small but certain flame of loving desire for God that still remains, express gratitude that your life with God was never your project to begin with. You can let down and simply be with God. You can be at home with yourself as well, not anxiously scanning the horizon for what's next. Reflect on any fruit you notice of God's deepening night work in you and thank God for it. In other words, cease striving and know that God is God (Psalm 46:10).

NIGHT VISION

This journey of descent is both necessary and initiated from God's loving desire for you. When you're doing day work in your formational journey you become confident that you clearly see God and know God. In truth, you have to start there. You can only begin to imagine God if you are able to make some concrete association to something or someone from your earthly experience. The only problem is that God is no "thing," and as such God is always beyond what we can conceive or imagine. The best we can do is envision God with an increasing approximation to the truth as we let go of our preconceptions and cherished categories.

So, the real gift of the dark night is that we set God free. In our earlier stages of our journey we put God in an attractively wrapped package. We begin to discover in the dark night that the One we seek is more than we can imagine; the Other we could never dream up; the Infinitely Beyond all our hearts can conceive. And though God is infinitely immense, we discover that we are deeply, personally and lavishly loved by this One in whom darkness is also light.

After twilight comes midnight. And after midnight comes the morning when this *noche oscura* is carried inside you into the dawn and rises up like a hymn: "The love of the Anointed is infinitely long, wide, high, and deep, surpassing everything anyone previously experienced" (Ephesians 3:19 *The Voice*).

What combination of emotions is stirred in you as you consider potential experiences of night work in your own life?

How is prayer changing during this season of life? Are there any hints that it is becoming more of a gift to receive and less of an effort or activity? What has that experience been like for you?

Can you identify with James? What "old ways" seem to not be working any longer? What activities do you need to release and be released from? If you consider that God might actually be in this phenomenon, how might God be at work?

Honestly, what's your heart toward God like right now? What do you most want in your relationship with God during this current season?

Take a few moments and intentionally release your spiritual journey, your progress or regress, your development and confusion to God. Thank him for working beneath the surface of your awareness to free you to love and be loved.

GOD ON THE LOOKOUT FOR YOU

In the first place, you should realize that, if the person is
seeking God, much more is her Beloved seeking her.

JOHN OF THE CROSS

A QUOTE AT THE BEGINNING OF this book is the original source of the book's inspiration and led to our writing *When Faith Becomes Sight*. In it William Barry suggests, "In order that an experience have a religious dimension two things are necessary: God who can be encountered directly and a person who is on the lookout for God." This declaration is stated so clearly and confidently. Is it *that* straightforward? If God can truly be encountered and we are looking for God, can we rest assured that we will meet God? Not only does the clarity of this straightforward statement appeal to us, the central truth it embodies corroborates our own quest to discover and experience the one we call God.

For all of our adult lives we have longed to assist others in encountering Christ as we have encountered him. Tapped by the Spirit as teenagers, in spite of the fact that neither of us had any religious upbringing to speak of, we met Jesus in separate and unique yet undeniable and profound ways, and our lives have forever been altered. From the onset of our encounters and really ever since, we have been on the lookout for this God who loves us and continually gives his life for us.

In the preface, we suggested three crucial capacities are needed for those looking for God's presence and activity in their lives. First, you must *recognize* God's presence by looking for God in particular phenomena, by looking through certain lenses—some conscious, some unconscious—and looking within your interior life for spiritual movement. As you gain proficiency in recognizing God's presence and involvement, that's *when faith becomes sight!* Then we recommended the need to *reflect* on your experience. Reflection is what brings home what you've encountered, as though fully digesting it as you savor the meaning and message. Finally, once you've recognized and reflected, you're more capable of *responding* with all of your heart in the ways you truly want to respond *and* in the ways God's inviting you to respond.

There's one final and reassuring theological reality that must be emphasized as we end. *While you endeavor to be on the lookout for God, be assured that God is on the lookout for you!* God, for all of your life, has kept his eye on you, aware of when you sit down and rise up, even knowing your thoughts from afar (Psalm 139:2). This God you seek has always been seeking you. The Trinity's patient and persistent desire is that you know God for who God truly is and become open to receiving God's gifts of unremitting love, forgiveness, and grace.

Not for one moment of your life have you been separated from God. Separation from God is an illusion! The divine presence is within and all around you. God isn't ever absent, but we all too often lack awareness of God's presence. Just as when children disobey or distance themselves from their parents, though this act causes relational strain, the parents never cease to be there and be for that child. So it is with God, the great lover of your soul, who is always and eternally with you, even when you doubt this love.

Yes, we wrote in the last chapter about night work, a time in our spiritual journey when God's presence and action are obscured from sight. That doesn't, however, indicate that God has left you. God simply rests behind a cloud of unknowing in order to awaken you from your sleep and instill a deeper hunger for Christ's love and presence.

When the prodigal son finally set out to return home, while still a long way off, he encountered his father looking for him, waiting for him, watching for him (Luke 15). In the same way, when you drift from God or even defiantly turn away, Love is patient and kind and continues to wait and watch for the first signs of your returning. Even more than that, the Spirit, who is your divine inheritance, works from the inside and "jealously desires" your heart to forever and always be God's home. Let us say it again: *While you endeavor to be on the lookout for God, be assured that God is on the lookout for you!*

To be on the lookout for God is no less than to be on the lookout for Love, for the Beloved, for our divine Lover. As we move progressively into our story, we discover what can only properly be called "the love story," a tale where our one true Love is amazingly in pursuit of us! As we conclude, our heartfelt prayer is that you find what you are looking for and what your soul longs for in your Beloved, the Trinity, who is always and forever looking for and pursuing you.

ACKNOWLEDGMENTS

WHERE DO WE BEGIN TO EXPRESS our heartfelt thanks to those who've made the publishing of this book possible? It seems especially important to begin with those who've trusted us to walk alongside them in their spiritual journeys—our directees. Whether you know it or not, we have learned a great deal from you. While sitting with you we've had the privilege of observing the gentle (and sometimes not-so gentle) disruptions of God in your life. This has strengthened our resolve to be on the lookout for God! We are blessed and honored to pray for you and listen to you with the ear of our heart. We hope the stories we've shared from some of your lives do honor to this sacred companionship we share.

We also are grateful for our Fall Creek Abbey spiritual directors' community! As of this year, we will have facilitated fourteen year-long cohorts, each one training individuals in the art and ministry of spiritual direction. These are our people and fellow learners to-gether! Of special note is our current and faithful Fall Creek Abbey peer supervision group, which meets monthly—Bev Gallagher, Karen Block, Dana Russo, Doug Haltom, Daniel Fuller, and Kim Parker—thank you for helping us to continue to grow our practice!

One other person deserves to be singled out. Nancy Campbell has been our spiritual director for more than seven years. Each month she faithfully greets us, along with her lovable three-legged pup, Shadow (a great name for the dog of a spiritual director and therapist), and listens to a lot of the same ramblings over and over again. And somehow Nancy always has something she hears and offers that we take with us to help us be more faithful in our Christ following. We speak of her throughout the book because Nancy is now part of the warp and woof of our spiritual lives.

Authors, like all others, don't live in a vacuum but in a community. These intimates of ours have become a rich compost of friends who regularly bless, support, challenge, and inspire us. We want to single out a few and express special thanks: Brent Croxton, Daniel and Kristin Fuller, Rob Pallikan, Mary and Tim Byers, Pam Sechrist, Megan and Nate Hershey, Melodie Asdell, Bev Gallagher, and Jim Matthies. We love, value, and cherish each of you.

And of course we are indebted to our publisher, InterVarsity Press. For years InterVarsity Press has published the books we love and read most. Now to be publishing with InterVarsity Press, in the Formatio line to boot, is a huge honor! We are extremely grateful to Jeff Crosby for his friendship and encouragement (he is a fellow Hoosier, after all), and to Cindy Bunch, our editor. Cindy passed our first draft of this book back to us with two exclamation points in her warm, positive email, and we thought we'd won the lottery of encouragement! She has offered wise suggestions and, as a spiritual director herself, has championed the value of writing from this point of view.

And finally we are compelled to thank our beautiful family. It's no small thing to raise four kids who grow into fine human beings who are kind, compassionate, and wise, and are working hard to make the world a better place. That describes all of them, including their spouses and significant others! We love you—Britt and Justin, Brandt and Laura, Bri and Dan, and Brooke. And then there are those little humans we are extremely fond of and call our "grands": Eli, Riley, Harper, Juniper, and Fern. You have made our world bright! To have you all no more than a bike ride away is like Mayberry, only much, much better! Thank you, dear family, for how you encourage us by your interest in our writing and by what we sense is genuine respect. We return it and are so grateful for you!

A WORD ABOUT EXPERIENCE

FOR MANY OF US WHO HAVE GROWN UP and been educated academically as well as spiritually within the late modern era, we have been heavily indoctrinated to mistrust all forms of subjectivity, especially the realm of experience and emotion. We were part of a ministry in our early years that crafted a diagram of a train engine, a cargo car, and caboose labeled "Fact," "Faith," and "Feeling." The train diagram illustrated the order to which we give authority. Needless to say, the domain of experience and the emotions were the weak little caboose, acknowledged yet forced to remain at the end of the line.

We are not suggesting that a robust and vital faith is solely or even primarily focused on our emotions. As a wise friend once said, "Emotions make terrible masters but important messengers." There is, however, a critical need for a more balanced approach; one that invites our whole person to come out from hiding behind a façade of sterile objectivity, sturdy precepts, and right doctrine into the only realm where we hope to find the *living* God—in our present, real, lived experience.

A conversion of heart is in order if we are to make progress in seeing, experiencing, and responding to the present reality of God, one that frees us from the suspicion of emotions, experience, and the messy complexities of life—in favor of reason. For too long, reason and objective truth have held a privileged position in our spiritual lives. Imagine what it would be like to attune to a more diverse means of encountering God. Would we not join the chorus of poets like Elizabeth Barrett Browning?

Earth's crammed with Heaven,

And every common bush afire with God;

But only he who sees, takes off his shoes.

Might we find that our experiences start to multiply—our faith becoming sight—and with renewed joy we set about exploring the real proportions of God and God's kingdom?

THE WESLEYAN QUADRILATERAL

One framework that we have found useful in navigating the need to balance our emotions and experience with our thinking and reasoning is the Wesleyan Quadrilateral. The Quadrilateral is described in *The Book of Discipline of the United Methodist Church*: "Wesley believed that the living core of the Christian faith was revealed in Scripture, illumined by tradition, vivified in personal experience and confirmed by reason."

Without engaging in a technical discussion about the Quadrilateral, we would like to suggest that for a Christ-follower, these four categories (Scripture, tradition, experience, and reason) are generally in play at any given moment and informing or influencing how we understand our encounters with God and respond to them. Imagine four legs of a table composed of the sacred words of Scripture, the historical and ongoing trajectory of tradition, the present storehouse of personal experience, and the ever-expanding gift of human reasoning. Can you see how solid the table is when all four legs are in place, grounding us fully in God's world?

It is our perspective that encountering the nearness and involvement of God is inherently phenomenological and therefore experience driven. It is our hope that by lengthening this table leg and drawing on the balancing properties of Scripture, tradition, and reason, we might be guided into a conversion of heart that more effectively engages God's heart toward us and our world.

THE UNIQUE STANCE
OF SPIRITUAL DIRECTION

WHEN FAITH BECOMES SIGHT offers in book form what we offer individuals in spiritual direction. This unique stance provides some of the perennial and nuanced points of view found in the spiritual direction tradition. Therefore the language and sensibilities found in the ministry of spiritual direction are woven throughout this book.

We acknowledge, however, that the term *spiritual direction* can be somewhat confusing if not misleading. Neither the person *receiving* direction (sometimes referred to as the directee) nor the one *serving* as the spiritual director are to be considered the originators of direction. The assumption in the background is that God alone is the true spiritual director. Gratefully, that enables us to relax and let go of any pressure to fabricate something or make things happen. God initiates, we simply respond.

Also, the term *spiritual* can be ambiguous. Paul in Acts 17:27-28 reminds us that God is not far from any of us and that "in him we live and move and exist." This perspective is echoed in the belief within spiritual direction that *all of life* is charged with the presence and activity of God and is therefore potential fodder for our spiritual human journey, becoming the nexus for encounter and transformation. In fact, we discover that the real genius in spiritual direction is that rather than turning away from life to find God, we're invited to turn full-faced toward our ordinary, beautiful, and messy life as the only place we can ever hope to find God. In other words, human experience becomes our ally, not our opponent.

If you are assisted by definitions, here's a brief description of spiritual direction that might help orient you as you start exploring what could feel like new terrain. Christian spiritual direction is

> help given by one believer to another that enables the latter to pay attention to God's personal communication to him or her, to respond to this personally communicating God, to grow in intimacy with this God, and to live out the consequences of the relationship.

In this book we offer several stories of people we've been honored to listen to as they seek to clothe their own experience of God with language. While these stories are *loosely* based on the true experiences of our directees, we've also left out, changed (including their names), or combined particular details in order to protect their identity. We hope these stories will benefit you if you're becoming interested in spiritual direction. These vignettes allow you to witness what spiritual direction is like. We also hope that these stories will be helpful to those already receiving and offering spiritual direction as you contemplate how to deepen your experiences in spiritual friendship and companionship.

Finally, we're not suggesting that this book is a replacement for receiving spiritual direction. Our aim is to provide the kind of support and guidance you might get from a human companion who embodies these qualities and skills. We hope it might even inspire you to find a spiritual director if you don't already have one!

NOTES

PREFACE

3   *find God in all things*: Ignatius of Loyola, as quoted by Kevin O'Brien, *The Ignatian Adventure* (Chicago: Loyola Press, 2011), 8.

CHAPTER 2: RECURRING THEMES AND SYMBOLS

22   *there is a vast interior space*: Jean-Marie Howe, *Secret of the Heart: Spiritual Being* (Collegeville, MN: Cistercian Publications, 2005), 73.

23   *Symbols and images serve to awaken*: Howe, *Secret of the Heart*, 74.

26   *Like many fly fishermen in Western Montana*: Norman Maclean, *A River Runs Through It* (Chicago: University of Chicago Press, 2017), 104

27   *adapted exercise*: David Benner, *Sacred Companions: The Gift of Spiritual Friendship and Direction* (Downers Grove, IL: InterVarsity Press, 2004), 118.

CHAPTER 3: TRANSCENDENT MOMENTS

35   *All shall be well*: Julian of Norwich, *Revelations of Divine Love* (Radford, VA: Wilder Publications, 2018), 80. Julian was an anchoress who lived in a simple cell adjacent to the church and devoted her entire life to prayer. As a young woman, Julian became gravely ill and experienced several "showings" or mystical revelations of Christ. Jesus spoke these reassuring words to her during one of her visions.

37   *Only wonder can comprehend*: Maximus the Confessor, quoted in Oliver Clement, *The Roots of Christian Mysticism* (Hyde Park, NY: New City Press, 2014), 27.

CHAPTER 4: SLENDER THREADS

39   *Several years ago, pastor and author Brian Zahnd*: Brian Zahnd, "Beauty Will Save the World," Apprentice Gather keynote message, May 20, 2018, www.youtube.com/watch?v=EPzPFzjMS6I.

42   *Of these three terms, synchronicity*: Carl Jung, *Man and His Symbols* (Garden City, NY: Doubleday, 1964), 211.

43   *this type of synchronicity has occurred*: Robert A. Johnson, *Balancing Heaven and Earth: A Memoir of Visions, Dreams, and Realizations* (New York: HarperOne, 1998), 70, Kindle.

      I think that the slender threads: Johnson, *Balancing Heaven and Earth*, 103.

50   *with expectation that the happenings*: Sam Keen, quoted in Gregg Levoy, *Callings: Finding and Following an Authentic Life* (New York: Crown Publishing, 1998), 100.

CHAPTER 5: THE FERTILE VOID

55   *meaning-making ceases and being begins*: Fritz Perls, quoted in Herb Stevenson, "Paradox: A Gestalt Theory of Change," Cleveland Consulting Group, July 15, 2004, www.clevelandconsultinggroup.com /pdfs/paradoxical_theory_of_change_iii.pdf.

CHAPTER 6: THE FACE OF GOD

67   *What comes to mind when we think about God*: A. W. Tozer, *The Knowledge of the Holy* (New York: HarperOne, 2009), 2.

69   *unhealthy God images amplify suffering and violence*: Matthias Beier "Healing Our God-Images," Spiritual Directors of Central Indiana, Spring 2015. Much of the content from his presentation is found in his book *A Violent God Image: An Introduction to the Work of Eugen Drewermann* (New York: Bloomsbury Academic, 2004).

CHAPTER 7: IMAGINING JESUS

79   *We live in an age of unbelief*: Ronald Rolheiser, *The Shattered Lantern: Rediscovering a Felt Presence of God* (New York: Crossroad, 2005), 17.

      a living person to whom we actually talk: Rolheiser, *Shattered Lantern*, 18.

84   *the ear of your heart*: Benedict of Nursia, *The Rule of St. Benedict in English* (Collegeville, MN: Liturgical Press, 1981), 15.

86   *Today this type of meditation is*: James Martin, *My Life with the Saints* (Chicago: Loyola Press, 2016), 94.

      visualizing an event as if making a movie: Kevin O'Brien, *The Ignatian Adventure* (Chicago: Loyola Press, 2011), 141.

87   *to see with the sight of the imagination*: Ignatius, quoted in James Martin, *My Life with the Saints* (Chicago: Loyola Press, 2016), 92.

CHAPTER 8: EXPECTATIONS AND ASSUMPTIONS

97   *law of retribution*: Mike Mason, *The Gospel According to Job: An Honest Look at Pain and Doubt from the Life of One Who Lost*

Everything (Wheaton, IL: Crossway Books, 1994). Mason explains how this ancient worldview (that is still very much in vogue) operated during the time that the book of Job, the oldest text in the Old Testament, was written, and why Job's story is such an affront to this law. Here a man who God defends as blameless and upright loses everything.

CHAPTER 9: THE HOLY FLAME

108 *sensus plenior:* A Latin phrase that means "fuller sense" or "fuller meaning." The term was coined by F. Andre Fernandez in 1927 but was popularized by Raymond E. Brown. Brown defines *sensus plenior* as "that additional, deeper meaning, intended by God but not clearly intended by the human author, which is seen to exist in the words of a biblical text (or group of texts, or even a whole book) when they are studied in the light of further revelation or development in the understanding of revelation." Raymond E. Brown, *The Sensus Plenior of Sacred Scripture* (Baltimore: St. Mary's University, 1955), 92.

The revealing work of the Holy Spirit: Michael Casey, *Sacred Reading* (Chicago: Triumph Books, 1996), 53.

We'd like to introduce four approaches: Casey, *Sacred Reading*, 52-57.

115 *Psalm 63:6-8 from the Benedictine Daily Prayer:* Maxwell E. Johnson, *Benedictine Daily Prayer: A Short Breviary*, 2nd ed. (Collegeville, MN: Liturgical Press, 2015), 1122.

CHAPTER 10: GOD'S BIG BOOK

120 *The Bible is God's little book:* J. Philip Newell, *Listening for the Heartbeat of God* (Mahwah, NJ: Paulist Press, 1997), 34.

123 *The heavens declare the glory of the Creator:* Quotes from the Psalms are from Nan Merrill, *Psalms for Praying: An Invitation to Wholeness* (New York: Continuum/Bloomsbury, 2006), 31, 40, 1, 174, 125.

124 *Are there any privileged places:* William A. Barry and William J. Connolly, *The Practice of Spiritual Direction* (New York: HarperOne, 2009), 54.

CHAPTER 11: (DIS)ORIENTATION

139 *It is precisely this noisy, chaotic mind:* Martin Laird, *Into the Silent Land: A Guide to the Practice of Contemplation* (London: Darton, Longman and Todd, 2006), 5.

140 *The action of God on our lives:* Margaret Silf, *Inner Compass: An Invitation to Ignatian Spirituality* (Chicago: Loyola Press, 2007), 86.

141   *prayer of examen*: For a guided exercise using the prayer of examen, as well as other contemplative spiritual practices, see "Contemplative Practices," Fall Creek Abbey, accessed March 29, 2019, www.fallcreek abbey.org/resources.

CHAPTER 12: BEFRIENDING DESIRE

150   *organ of desire*: Bernard of Clairvaux, cited in Michael Casey, *Athirst for God* (Kalamazoo, MI: Cistercian Publications, 1987), 66-67.

153   *wants are the bands and cement between God and us:* Thomas Traherne, *Centuries of Meditations* (Scotts Valley, CA: CreateSpace, 2012), 1.44,51.

        Origen consistently preferred the use of eros: Philip Sheldrake, *Befriending Our Desires* (London: Darton, Longman and Todd, 2001), 53. Origen of Alexandria (c. 184–c. 253) was an early Christian scholar, ascetic, and theologian, as well as a prolific writer. He wrote roughly two thousand treatises in multiple branches of theology, including textual criticism, biblical exegesis and biblical hermeneutics, homiletics, and spirituality, and was described as "the greatest genius the early church ever produced."

154   *God's yearning for us precedes*: Janet Ruffing, *Spiritual Direction: Beyond the Beginnings* (Mahwah, NJ: Paulist Press, 2000), 14.

CHAPTER 13: ENDLESSLY INVENTIVE RESISTANCE

160   *"Endlessly Inventive Evasions"*: Janet Ruffing, *Spiritual Direction: Beyond the Beginnings* (Mahwah, NJ, Paulist Press, 2000).

161   *not something to be condemned or pitied*: William A. Barry and William J. Connolly, *The Practice of Spiritual Direction* (New York: HarperOne, 2009), 94.

168   *We can't resist a vacuum*: Sue Pickering, *Spiritual Direction: A Practical Introduction* (Norwich, UK: Hymns Ancient and Modern, 2008), 159.

CHAPTER 14: ESSENCE AND ILLUSION

172   *There is only one problem on which*: Thomas Merton, *New Seeds of Contemplation* (New York: New Directions, 2007), 36.

        the person we would like to be: David Benner, *The Gift of Being Yourself* (Downers Grove, IL: InterVarsity Press, 2015), 80.

174   *There is no deep knowing of God*: Benner, *Gift of Being Yourself*, 20.

182   *I came to you late, O Beauty*: Augustine of Hippo, "I Came to You Late," *Catholic.net*, accessed March 29, 2019, http://catholic.net/op /articles/1339/cat/1230/i-came-to-you-late.html.

     We do not find our true self by seeking it: Benner, *The Gift of Being Yourself*, 91.

CHAPTER 15: NIGHT WORK

188   *Lonely is this city that once bustled with life*: The Scripture in "Working in the Dark" is from *The Voice*.

189   *two doctors of the interior life*: If you are interested in reading more about these two spiritual advisers consider Thomas Dubay, *Fire Within: St. Teresa of Avila, St. John of the Cross, and the Gospel on Prayer* (San Francisco: Ignatius Press, 1989).

190   *noche oscura*: John of the Cross, quoted in Gerald May, *The Dark Night of the Soul: A Psychiatrist Explores the Connection Between Darkness and Spiritual Growth* (New York: HarperCollins, 2005), 26.

191   *Following Gerald May's synthesis*: May, *Dark Night of the Soul*, 138-41.

193   *The dark night is a profoundly good thing*: May, *Dark Night of the Soul*, 4.

     John Coe offers a wonderful illustration: John Coe, "Musings on the Dark Night of the Soul: Insights from St. John of the Cross on a Developmental Spirituality," *Journal of Psychology and Theology* 28, no. 4 (2000): 293-307.

194   *There are four discernible phases*: Bernard of Clairvaux, quoted in May, *Dark Night of the Soul*, 99-100.

CONCLUSION

202   *In order that an experience have a religious dimension*: William Barry, *Spiritual Direction and the Encounter with God* (Mahwah, NJ: Paulist Press, 2005), 37.

APPENDIX 1

208   *Wesley believed that the living core*: Ted A. Campbell, *Wesley and the Quadrilateral: Renewing the Conversation* (Nashville: Abingdon Press, 1997), 9.

APPENDIX 2

210   *Christian spiritual direction is*: William A. Barry and William J. Connolly, *The Practice of Spiritual Direction* (San Francisco: HarperOne, 2009), 48.

FALL CREEK ABBEY
a retreat house in Indianapolis renewing the contemplative spirit

Fall Creek Abbey is an urban retreat house in Indianapolis thoughtfully designed for those seeking to reconnect their hearts with the heart of God. When someone walks through the doors into the Abbey, it's not uncommon for them to pause and want to name what they're feeling: the sensation of peace, quiet, welcome, and simple beauty. Many who come are seeking a sanctuary where they will be undisturbed and find rest in a setting that is supportive and nurturing.

"Our great joy at Fall Creek Abbey is to live a life that is right-sized for our season; one where small things are cherished, slowness is a virtue, and solitude is a welcomed relief from a busy, noisy world."

This was a major theme when God prompted Beth and David to launch the Abbey in 2011 (formerly called Sustainable Faith Indy). As its hosts, they've currently welcomed over seven thousand guests to this still point in their city where individuals can step away from their responsibilities and reorient their heart to the loving heart of God.

As trained spiritual directors, David and Beth spend a good deal of their days sitting with women and men who want to hear God's voice of invitation and respond wholeheartedly. In addition, they speak regularly at workshops and conferences, design and facilitate group retreats, and lead the Fall Creek Abbey School of Spiritual Direction, where they train individuals in the art and ministry of spiritual companioning.

Beth is the author of several books, including *Starting Something New: Spiritual Direction for Your God-given Dream*, in which she tells the story of Fall Creek Abbey. David has his MDiv from Trinity Evangelical Divinity School and, in addition to his other work, continues his private practice in career counseling with Direction 4 Life Work.

For more information about Fall Creek Abbey and the Boorams go to fallcreekabbey.org.